W9-BQY-447

LINCOLN CHRISTIAN COLLEGE AND SEMINARY

Peaceable Witness Among Muslims

Peaceable Witness Among Muslims

Gordon D. Nickel

Foreword by Calvin E. Shenk

Herald
Press

Scottdale, Pennsylvania
Waterloo, Ontario

Canadian Cataloging-in-Publication Data
Nickel, Gordon
  Peaceable Witness among Muslims
Includes bibliographical references.
ISBN -08361-9105-6
1. Missions to Muslims. 2. Mennonites—missions. 3. Anabaptists—
Doctrines. I Title
BV2625.N42 1999   266′.0088′2971   c99-931998-1

The paper used in this publication is recycled and meets the minimum re-
quirements of American National Standard for Information Sciences—
Permanence of Paper for Printed Library Materials, ANSI Z39.48-1984.

All Bible quotations are used by permission, all rights reserved, and except
when otherwise indicated are from the *The Holy Bible, New International
Version*, copyright © 1973, 1978, 1984 International Bible Society, Zondervan
Bible Publishers

PEACEABLE WITNESS AMONG MUSLIMS
Copyright © 1999 by Herald Press, Waterloo, Ont. N2L 6H7
        Published simultaneously in the United States by Herald Press,
        Scottdale, Pa. 15683. All rights reserved
Library of Congress Catalog Number: 99-073585
International Standard Book Number: 0-8361-9105-6
Printed in the United States of America
Book design by Michael A. King, Pandora Press U.S., in consultation with Jim
Butti, Herald Press
Cover design by Jim Butti, Herald Press

08 07 06 05 04 03 02 01 00 99 10 9 8 7 6 5 4 3 2 1

To order or request information, please call
1-800-759-4447 (individuals); 1-800-245-7894 (trade).
Website: www.mph.org

To Peter Hamm,
Secretary for Asia,
Mennonite Brethren Missions/Services

99703

Contents

Foreword

For many Christians Islam is an enemy. Often Islam is defined by ways it differs from or opposes Christian faith. Christians resist Islam's claim to have fulfilled and gone beyond Christianity. Some Christians are troubled by political forms of Islam which espouse values antithetic to traditional Christian ones. For other Christians, Islam as a missionary religion is in competition with Christian witness. Unfortunately such partial perspectives of Islam engender fear and hatred and poison relationships between Christians and Muslims.

Peaceable Witness among Muslims is a refreshing alternative. Nickel's recognition of the variety in Islam is a corrective to monolithic views of Islam. Nickel neither idealizes nor denigrates Islam. He writes with honesty and integrity, in a tone that commends empathetic understanding.

Clearly the author's sensitivity reflects firsthand acquaintance with a variety of Muslims, including some who have become disciples of Jesus. I welcome this because my own perception of Islam has been similarly influenced by Muslim students in Ethiopia and by Ethiopian Muslims who have become Jesus' followers. The Meserete Kristos (Mennonite) Church in Ethiopia has dozens of members from Islamic background. Former Muslims serve in church administration. Two of five church leaders imprisoned during the Marxist period were from Islamic background.

For Nickel witness includes fairness in portraying Muslims, cultural sensitivity, person-centeredness, engaging Islamic concepts, and responding respectfully to issues Muslims raise. The book is a rich combination of theology and testimony. Hopeful yet realistic, Nickel believes Muslims can become disciples of Jesus Christ. He avoids sloganeering about Islamic evangelism and criticizes inappropriate missiology in Muslim contexts. Showing that Christian conviction can encompass affirmation of Islamic values, he models confidence without dogmatism.

9

Nickel warns against cultural imposition or judgmentalism. He recommends a clear Christology and conversation without presuppositions. Witness to Muslims should model holistic concern, including compassionate service, friendship, dialogue, sacrifice for another, and reconciliation. Since a great stumbling block for Muslims is the cross, because it models the vulnerability of God, it is crucial that Christians model and interpret the cross. This will include repentance for ways the cross has been misused in aggression against Muslims.

One of the greatest strengths of this book is the author's seriousness about explicitly integrating Anabaptist concepts of peace, suffering, servanthood, love of enemy, and criticism of political power. He cautions against a success orientation to witness.

Nickel calls for a peace which is not marginal or optional. Peace is the heart of the gospel. Peace is especially important when one recalls that Christian encounters with Muslims often negated God's love. Peace is also in contrast to some Islamic efforts to spread Islam by power, force, defeat of enemy. When gospel peace is practiced in Islamic contexts, it highlights the contrast between Christian and Muslim worldviews.

Nickel believes witness should also include Anabaptist concerns for discipleship, church formation, vulnerability, and sacrifice. Nickel emphasizes quality of church life as integral to witness. My experience in the Middle East confirms his concern for needed sensitivity to local church leadership, especially when it is difficult for local churches to integrate local converts into pre-existing churches. Nickel's emphasis on pastoral concern for new believers is crucial.

Nickel understands that witness to Muslims has spiritual as well as sociological and theological dimensions. He emphasizes weapons of the Spirit but is cautious about language of spiritual warfare. He reminds the reader that one weapon of the Spirit is the gospel of peace. We should not demonize Islam but emphasize the love of Jesus Christ in all our relationships with Muslims. For this, patience, perseverance, and hope are required. Faithfulness is more important than predicting success.

Some years ago I asked a once-Muslim student of mine why he had become a Christian. After a brief pause he replied, "The God I knew as Allah came close in Jesus." The Christian hope is built on God coming close in Jesus Christ. This book is an excellent resource for helping Christians witness to Muslims that God has come close in Jesus Christ.

—*Calvin E. Shenk*
Professor of Religion, Eastern Mennonite University, Harrisonburg,
Virginia; and Research Scholar, Tantur Ecumenical Institute, Jerusalem

Preface

Confident defenseless witness to Jesus Christ. Mission commitment willing to suffer and die for the sake of the gospel, but never to hurt or kill.

The genius of the early church was ability to hold together open proclamation of the good news with a peaceable manner of living and speaking. This beautiful characteristic has radiated out at many times and many places in the history of the church. True, it has often been obscured and repudiated when Christians have justified the use of physical force to spread or maintain religion. But the first three peaceable centuries of the church's existence are a treasure for all Christians to cherish.

Has this genius of peaceable witness been applied to the encounter with Islam? Islam is a post-Constantinian religion. It arose at a time when Christians had grown accustomed to mixing political power with faith in Jesus. Islam burst on the world in a remarkable military conquest which soon extended from Spain to India. The story of its first centuries is a striking contrast to the humble origins and peaceful early spread of Christianity. Has Islam ever had the opportunity to experience the Christianity of that early peaceful period?

The Anabaptists of sixteenth-century Europe called for a return to pre-Constantinian Christian faith and practice. They believed in the power of the gospel and boldly took that message throughout Catholic, Lutheran, and Reformed dominions. But they also took a stand against the use of physical force in matters of faith. The lessons from the Anabaptist heritage are available for application to the Muslim context. How might they look if applied there?

A recent Anabaptist story provides a quick sketch. In 1998, Mennonite Central Committee sent Roy and Maren Hange to Qom, Iran, in a student exchange. Roy was the first resident Christian to study at the Imam

Khomeini Education and Research Institute. Maren was the first Christian at the main women's university in Qom. Roy and Maren studied the Qur'an and Islam. And Roy also taught a group of Muslim scholars who studied Christianity and other religions. Roy took the freedom to introduce these scholars to John Howard Yoder's book, *The Politics of Jesus*.

Roy and Maren were vulnerable in the city where Imam Khomeini had studied and taught—and where today students from around the world prepare for the Islamic revolution. The couple entered Qom as learners about Islam. At the same time, they went with the conviction that the person of Jesus is essential to the encounter with Islam. Roy taught Yoder's book to the Shi'ite scholars to share with them "a way of being political that is not controlling and is central to who Jesus was and the new kind of community begun in Christianity." He believed a fresh dialogue between Western Christians and Iranian Muslims must begin with a full picture of Jesus, especially his death on the cross.

These chapters attempt to describe the integration of faithful proclamation and peaceable method and to apply that style of witness to the Muslim context. This is not a book about Islam or about the theological issues between gospel and Islam. Such details as are given about Islam are all available from academic study of what Muslims have written about their history and faith. The earliest sources for the history of Islam are accounts of the raids of the Prophet (*Maghazi*). The contents of the Qur'an, *Sira* (Muslim biography of Muhammad) and *Hadith* (traditions of the Prophet) are open to all readers, as are the classical Muslim histories of the Islamic conquests.

If the Muslim story includes the use of physical force, this is not something seen by most Muslims as negative. The way this activity is judged depends on the standard set alongside it. There is a Muslim critique of Christianity, developed by authors such as Fazlur Rahman, which judges Jesus to have been weak and incomplete because he did not seize political power and thus achieve success as an earthly ruler. Roy Hange encountered this critique in Qom, where students of religion prepare to change the political face of the world. Contemporary revivalist movements in Islam are happy with the portrait of Muhammad as both prophet and warrior.

On the other hand, if the behavior of Jesus is treated as the standard, a criterion is set up whereby wielders of the sword are inevitably criticized. Michael Cook, in his academic treatment of the life of Muhammad, writes about the Prophet's use of armed confrontation to bring in the way of God. "These ideas are not notably eirenic," Cook observes, "and to anyone brought up on the New Testament they will seem very alien."

This book had its origin in a series of enjoyable experiences. I gained a deep appreciation for the Anabaptist heritage from working with Harold Jantz at the *Mennonite Brethren Herald* in Winnipeg, Manitoba, and from studying at the Mennonite Brethren Biblical Seminary in Fresno, California.

When I then took up the academic study of Islam at the School of Oriental and African Studies in London, England, I noticed that the Muslim accounts of the life of the Prophet of Islam set up a striking contrast to the New Testament accounts of the life of Jesus. Later, as Gwen and I worked as missionaries in Pakistan, we learned to understand Islam as believers themselves express it, and to hear the heartbeat of a local church in the midst of Muslims. I realized that there are many others who appreciate the contrasts between the gospel and Islam.

I also became acquainted with a number of fascinating stories of peaceable gospel witness among Muslims, which I try to integrate into these chapters. Finally, there arose a need in MBMS International to sketch out an approach to Muslim ministries. As I wrote the manuscript, I tried out some of the ideas on students of mission at Bethany Bible Institute.

Muslim ministry was made a viable option for Gwen and me by my parents, Dan and Helen Nickel, who pioneered a Muslim focus under MBMS International in Indonesia and India. I am also thankful to MBMS International for giving me time to write while I was serving as a resource missionary for Muslim ministries. MBMSI contributed toward costs of production.

Particular thanks go to Peter Hamm, Secretary for Asia for MBMSI when Gwen and I became missionaries in 1986. Peter encouraged us strongly and allowed us to get a start in the academic study of Islam. In recent years, Dave Dyck, MBMSI Director of Programs, has given supervision and support. David Shenk of Eastern Mennonite Missions has also affirmed the impulses behind this book.

—*Gordon Nickel*
  Calgary, Alberta

Peaceable Witness
Among Muslims

Chapter One

Singing above the Azaan

To serve Jesus among Muslims is a privilege and one of the greatest adventures life on earth has to offer. Muslim people represent a fascinating variety of personality traits and cultural traditions. Getting to know them as friends means coming in contact with their sophisticated, highly developed religion. Observing their faith and life leads to admiration for many expressions of piety, commitment, and discipline.

The great work of gospel witness among Muslims challenges the resources of the Christian messenger. The Muslim context is like no other—both in the way it draws out the gospel message and in the way it responds to the message once heard.

When a message of good news and a challenging context come together, the Christian messenger can learn some important lessons. The Muslim setting repeatedly raises the question of whether the manner of Christian witness matches the content of the gospel message. It also teaches Christians to take a long-term view. Hendrick Kraemer wrote, after serving Jesus among Muslims in Indonesia, "Through all the ages Islam has been, in relation to the missionary efforts of the Christian Church, the teacher of patience" (1938:353).

Early in the course of our ministry as a family to Muslims in Karachi, Pakistan, we were asked to represent Canada in an international Christmas program. My wife and I chose to sing a gentle song from our ethnic past, "Oh come, little children." Our own three children were young, and there was no sound system to use, but the stone walls of old St. Andrews Cathedral caught the sound of our song and bounced it back to the gathering. The windows of the church were open all around the edge of the sanctuary, letting in the fresh evening air.

> O come, little children, O come one and all.
> To Bethlehem hasten—in manger so small
> God's Son for a gift has been sent you this night,
> To be your Redeemer, your joy and delight. . . .

Suddenly the amplifier of the mosque across the street clicked on. Out of its horn loudspeakers came the Muslim call to prayer—the *adhan*—summoning the neighborhood to the evening prayer time. The

God's Son for a gift has been sent you this night,
To be your Redeemer, your joy and delight. . . .

Suddenly the amplifier of the mosque across the street clicked on. Out of its horn loudspeakers came the Muslim call to prayer—the *adhan*—summoning the neighborhood to the evening prayer time. The amplified Arabic words entered through the open windows of the church and filled the stone sanctuary right up to the aging rafters, completely drowning out our gentle song. The Christmas program audience could see that we were singing, but they couldn't hear a sound we were making.

Song of Joyous Witness

That experience of being physically overpowered in a Muslim setting led us gradually toward reflections on the relationship of the gospel to Islam. Gwen and I knew the beauty of the gospel "song" and were committed to passing it on to others. How could we learn to sing in a way which matched the song?

Islam is a powerful religious force in the world. It has its own energetic concept of *da'wa* or missionary outreach. Gospel witness in Islamic contexts today is often made from a position of considerable weakness. The appeal of the adhan—the "call of the minaret" as Kenneth Cragg called it—is powerful indeed. Five times each day in all Muslim countries the call to prayer bears witness to Allah and the Prophet of Islam in a confident and compelling way. The call constitutes an attractive challenge to humanity to be disciplined in the practices of religion. It includes in its text a promise of success for performing the Muslim prayers regularly. It repeats with boldness and pride, *Allaho-akbar*—"God is greater." The call proclaims a transcendent, inscrutable God who holds every human being accountable for his or her actions. The sound of the adhan drowns out all other appeals in the Muslim world.

By contrast, the Christmas song we were singing in the cathedral was an invitation to a stable in Bethlehem, where God himself appears humble and meek in the weakness of human flesh. He takes on himself the helpless form of a baby. He makes himself vulnerable. The incarnation is part of God's magnificent plan to reconcile the world to himself. His plan includes providing people with forgiveness of sins through the sacrifice of Jesus Christ on the cross. He promises eternal life and many other blessings to the people of the world. That is good news for people from all cultural and religious backgrounds! It is a message which begs to be told.

If Christ is what Christ is, he must be uttered. If Islam is what Islam is, that "must" is irresistible. Wherever there is misconception, witness must penetrate; wherever there is the obscuring of the beauty of the Cross, it must be unveiled; wherever persons have missed God in Christ, he must be brought to them again. (Cragg 1985a:304)

The gospel is a "song" of great beauty. But how often have Muslims been able to hear the good news as it really is? How many times have they perhaps rather experienced Christian witness as a cultural imposition from outside, or a pronouncement of judgment on them and their beliefs, or as fighting words of polemic which pressure them to admit they are wrong? In the Muslim world, is it not possible that some have thought of the gospel as the religious counterpart to the political aggression which Christians have shown during such times as the Crusades, the European colonial expansion, and the 1991 Persian Gulf War?

Anglican missionary Temple Gairdner was perhaps thinking of such questions when he wrote from Cairo in the early 1900s, "We need the *song* note in our message to the Muslims . . . not the dry cracked note of disputation, but the song of joyous witness, tender invitation" (Chapman 1995:297).

Offense of Loudspeakers

When we hear the impressive call of the minaret and feel the attraction it has for more than a billion people in the world, we sometimes wonder how the gospel can gain a hearing. When work challenges our physical resources and it is not easy to accomplish our goals, we may begin to grasp at keys or shortcuts or quick solutions. The loudspeaker represents advances in technology which can prove very helpful in the work of gospel witness. But the loudspeaker can also be a symbol of the temptation to place trust in technique or technology or other physical means to accomplish a task which is essentially spiritual in nature.

The nature of the gospel message itself encourages us to question whether we will gain a suitable hearing by blasting it through bigger loudspeakers. The appeal of the gospel song is not physical but rather spiritual. It is the gospel of peace, and as such must be related peaceably. The picture of the suffering servant in Isaiah gives us an example of ministry in the peaceable style:

He will bring justice to the nations.
He will not shout or cry out, or raise his voice in the streets.
A bruised reed he will not break,

and a smoldering wick he will not snuff out.
In faithfulness he will bring forth justice;
he will not falter or be discouraged till he establishes justice on
earth. (Isa. 42:1-4)

God's servant will certainly complete the assignment which God gives
him, and he will do it through full trust in the power of God alone.

Beyond this is the question of whether people from any culture
really respond meaningfully to a message pushed at them by physical
means. Eugene Nida, an expert in cross-cultural communication, notes
the damage technology can do in Aboriginal tribes: "The use of the
loudspeaker tends to destroy the sanctity of religion, and the offense of
booming the message into one's home, especially when it is not wanted,
seems the height of inconsiderateness, if not of insolence" (1960:172).

If Christians are going to be able to sing above the *adhan*—to gain a
hearing for the good news—it will not be because we overpower the
Muslim call to prayer by sheer volume. It will be because the song about
Jesus which God has given us to sing is from above, and because the way
in which we sing matches the message. It will be because the song draws
out of the hearer a ready recognition of its truth, and a free response to
believe and follow.

Compelled by Love

This is a book about singing. A beautiful song begs to be sung. The
singer needs no other motivation. She simply seeks to sing the song in
such a way that its full beauty can be heard.

Christians tell the good news about Jesus Christ among Muslims
because witness is an expression of the inner law of their lives. The Holy
Spirit is the driving force behind their mission activities. When Jesus
said to his disciples, "You shall be my witnesses," he gave them a promise they could trust. Their desire to share their faith with others came
from a sense of gratitude to God for what he has done for them. The appropriate Christian motivation for gospel witness, according to Paul, is
"Christ's love" (2 Cor. 5:14). Gospel messengers will seek to communicate the gospel effectively. But their motivation cannot be "success" in
human terms.

"No Christian mission is constituted in its success, and none, therefore, is invalidated by numerical failure. . . . there is a Christian obligation to Islam that neither begins nor ends in how Muslims respond. It is
rooted in the nature of Christ and his Gospel" (Cragg 1985a:304-5). It is
the Muslim context in particular which challenges Christians—

especially from Western countries—to examine their success orientation and to make certain that their motivation goes beyond merely cultural values.

All Global Directions

Muslim ministry is not a cultural enterprise in which people from North America and Europe attempt to impose their home cultures on people in the Middle East, Asia, and Africa. First of all, the gospel is not a product of Western culture. Its original cultural setting is the Semitic milieu of Palestine, near the crossroads of Asia and Africa—the "Bethlehem" of our Christmas song. The goal of gospel witness is to make the good news about Jesus understandable and relevant in all cultural settings. And the cultural setting of the Gospels has more in common with many Muslim countries than it does with post-Enlightenment Europe and North America.

Secondly, the movement of Muslim ministry is not only west to east, though Christian workers from Europe and North America will likely continue to serve in Muslim countries. Rather, the movement of Muslim ministry is in all global directions, including east to west and south to north. Lamin Sanneh, Michael Nazir Ali, and Patrick Sookhdeo are only three among a growing number of leaders from the two-thirds world who are showing the way in Muslim ministry out of an intimate experience of Islam. Stories in subsequent chapters will give more examples of this trend.

Similarly, gospel witness among Muslims is not part of a political agenda. Here the Muslim context challenges us to keep our loyalties straight. For more than 1,000 years people in the West have viewed Muslims in the Middle East as their enemies. Muslim armies conquered Spain already in the seventh century A.D. and fought as far north as France. The Ottoman Turks conquered Constantinople (now Istanbul) in 1453 and moved across Yugoslavia to the gates of Vienna by the time of the Protestant Reformation. European powers in turn conquered and dominated much of the Middle East, North Africa, and Asia during the colonial era. Even today, after the disintegration of the Soviet Union, Islam is sometimes characterized as an evil power opposing American interests in the world. The Persian Gulf War gave vivid examples of how quickly North American Christians can approve war against Middle Eastern nations.

Christians who want the good news of Jesus Christ and the blessings of salvation to reach all people cannot, however, merely follow national feelings as their approach toward Muslims. If it indeed happens that a Muslim nation becomes a political enemy of our own country, then the command of Jesus becomes our rule, "Love your enemies, do good to those who hate you, bless those who curse you, pray for those who mistreat you" (Luke 6:27, 28).

The mission of God to save a lost world—including Muslims—simply takes precedence over national goals of defense or domination. Here God himself has set the example. When we were God's enemies, Paul writes, God demonstrated his love for us by sending his own dear Son to die for us (Rom. 5:8).

Resources of the Church

The biblical teachings on mission provide us with a strong foundation for faithful ministry to Muslims. Each chapter to follow begins by affirming biblical materials which provide a basis for each theme.

Additional resources to strengthen that foundation come from the church. We are blessed today with a wealth of materials written out of experiences of personal contact with Muslims during the past 200 years. The writers come from many church traditions and mission organizations. Some of the greatest mission statesmen from Europe and North America have been missionaries who worked in Muslim contexts. And some of the finest church leaders in the two-thirds world today are Muslim converts who have much wisdom to share. The end of the twentieth century seems to be the occasion of a rich harvest of insight. God has given us these resources for a purpose. The strongest influences on my thinking from this treasure trove will soon become clear.

Unfortunately, in many of the best-known stories of Christian-Muslim encounter, Christians did not display God's love for the world. Those stories should certainly lead Christians to confession and repentance. But we should not let those stories obscure the lesser-known stories of obedience which encourage us toward peaceable gospel witness.

In my references at the end of the book, I have tried to draw attention to some of the best articles and books available today on each of the themes. Where I have only been able to introduce a line of thought, these resources often develop the theme more fully.

Peace Teaching and Reconciliation

Among the resources of the church for ministry to Muslims are insights arising from the Anabaptist movement of the sixteenth century.

My experience has been that Muslim ministry becomes much more fascinating when a commitment to Christ and a love for Muslims come together with lessons from the Anabaptist heritage.

In the following chapters, insights from the Anabaptist story are offered for several reasons. One reason is that this is my own heritage as a member of the Mennonite Brethren Church. A second reason is that the Anabaptist heritage presents insights which are needed in the area of Muslim ministry and yet have not often been highlighted for use by the gospel messenger. Sometimes, it may be, these insights have been intentionally neglected. In mission thinking in general, it has been customary in North America and Europe to dismiss the peace teachings of the Anabaptists and other peace churches as marginal and optional. But Christians from the growing churches of the two-thirds world are now making it clear that peace teaching and reconciliation ministries are a vital part of Christian faithfulness and are desperately needed around the world (Lawton 1997:44).

The themes of peace and reconciliation need to be highlighted in every setting because they are at the heart of the gospel message. In the Muslim context, however, these themes draw special attention to themselves because of the way in which Islam was originally formulated in its Scripture, in the biography and traditions of its Prophet, and in the concurrent history of military conquest.

A third reason for highlighting these themes is the actions of the past which have misrepresented the gospel. When Christians from Europe and North America have come into contact with Muslims, they have often associated the cross with an aggressive, warlike approach. Christians today have the responsibility to let Muslims know the Christian message as the gospel of peace.

There are other more recent indications that an emphasis on peace teaching and reconciliation is crucial in ministry to Muslims. When Lutheran missiologist Mark Thomsen applies a "missiology of the cross" to witness among Muslims, it is interesting that he contrasts unfavorably the teachings of Martin Luther with those of Menno Simons (an influential Dutch Anabaptist leader). The writings of Kenneth Cragg also indicate a need. No one is better known than this Anglican bishop for giving Islam a sympathetic hearing from the point of view of a commitment to the gospel. When he approaches the question of "Muhammad and the Christian," he bases his judgment of Islam's Prophet on a gospel understanding of the use of physical force.

Two events of the 1990s highlight contradictions in the Western Christian attitude toward the Muslim world. On the one hand, during the 1991 Persian Gulf War a large number of Western Christians endorsed national foreign policy decisions which resulted in the killing of Muslims in Iraq. On the other hand, after the Gulf War, other Western Christians attempted to rally Christians in Europe and North America to ask forgiveness for the atrocities committed during the Crusades 900 years ago. Their Reconciliation Walk, culminating in July 1999, was an act of repentance along the routes the Crusaders took on their violent way to the holy land. This juxtaposition raises the question of what the gospel of peace means for our relationship with Muslims.

If there are resources in the Anabaptist heritage which can prove helpful in these discussions, they should be offered with gratefulness. The Anabaptist experience can be a source of encouragement for gospel messengers, given the difficulties of ministry among Muslims.

Experience in Asia

Mennonite Brethren (MB) mission during the past 100 years has not had much to do with witness among Muslims. However, there was significant promise for this ministry early in that period. One of the first locations of MB mission work was the Muslim kingdom of Hyderabad in India. And the first MB workers there made a witness to Muslims before World War I. Missionary J. H. Pankratz and national evangelist J. S. Levi baptized a Muslim who had turned toward Christ through their witness. In fact, it was the uproar over this baptism which caused the ruler of the city to relocate the MB missionaries to another—Hindu—part of town (D. Nickel 1985:14). Missionaries read that relocation as the closing of one door and the opening of another. They opted to concentrate their mission efforts on the more receptive Hindu population.

Another interesting story comes from the southern republics of the former Soviet Union. Herman Jantzen was born into an MB family which in the late nineteenth century moved into what is now Kyrgyzstan. While working as a forester, Herman got to know the languages and cultures of the Muslim groups in southern Russia. After he was born again in 1910, he led many Muslims to Christ and baptism in the years just before and after the First World War. Inspired by his example, Heinrich Voth and others developed a vision for outreach to Muslims in the 1970s. They began translating the Bible into Kyrgyz, Kazakh, and Uzbek. A breakthrough in their ministry came in the 1990s, when newly converted Kyrgyz began witnessing to their own people.

In recent years, workers under MBMS International have begun a witness to Muslims in Afghanistan (1969), Indonesia (1975), India

(1984), and Pakistan (1988). When Dan and Helen Nickel went to India in 1984 to focus on gospel witness among Muslims, they intentionally located in Malakpet, the neighborhood where MBs had begun their witness. Hyderabad is no longer ruled by a Muslim, and the Muslims of the Hyderabad region find themselves a minority community alongside the Christians, amid a huge Hindu majority.

Because Muslims do not exercise political control, there is greater freedom for the national MB church there to share the gospel with Muslims. An Indian convert from Islam, John Mahboob, conducted a Bible correspondence course for Muslims under the India MB Conference from 1985 to 1997.

I have indicated this limited denominational experience through the title of this chapter. *Azaan* is the way Muslims in South Asia pronounce the Arabic word adhan. The approach of this book is certainly influenced by the experience of witness among Muslims in Central and South Asia.

Beauty of the Gospel

When we get to know Muslims and their faith, we notice that part of the history of the Prophet of Islam which Muslims recount is a story of violence. This violence is written into the Scripture of Islam itself—the Qur'an. The example of the Prophet and the verses of the Qur'an on this theme will continue to be the backdrop of actual violence in the name of Islam as we enter the third millenium. When the life of Jesus Christ is brought into this context, his teachings and actions are highlighted in a remarkable way. That aspect of the gospel draws attention toward itself by contrast, as if God is giving Christians a special chance to appreciate the beauty of the gospel.

Part of the great privilege of gospel witness among Muslims is that the Muslim context itself draws out of the gospel many emphases which we may not have noticed before. Samuel Zwemer noted after many years of witness in the Middle East that the cross of Christ takes on greater and greater significance. The missionary among Muslims "is driven daily to deeper meditation on this mystery of redemption and to a stronger conviction that here is the very heart of our message and our mission" (Chapman 1995:338).

Such privileges help sustain the Christian worker in the face of the more challenging aspects of gospel witness among Muslims. Serving Jesus among Muslims is a wonderful adventure, but only if done in an attitude of faithful ministry. Kraemer discovered that the prime condition of the approach to Islam is faith, hope, love and endurance that never wear out, and of which love is "the greatest of all" (1 Cor. 13). By its stubborn rigidity and pride, implied in its being the deification of group solidarity, Islam is a trying religion to converse with. . . . Only if faith, hope, love and endurance, however much tempted, ever and again break through triumphantly, will he perform his missionary obligation well. As this is the prime condition of all missionary approach to Islam, there follows from it the conclusion that the Christian Church must stand behind her ambassadors in this difficult field with prayer and loving remembrance to a degree quite different from what is practiced now. (1938: 354-5)

Chapter Two

Bearing Witness to Christ

One of the most remarkable stories in Christian mission is the witness of the women of the Anabaptist movement. They courageously confessed their faith and spread it at great risk among relatives and neighbors.

During the sixteenth century, governments all over Europe routinely exiled or executed Anabaptists. In the Württemberg region of Germany, however, the government treated married women differently out of regard for their little children. But the authorities considered the witness of these women so contagious that they chained the women in their homes. "This, of course," notes historian Wolfgang Schäufele, "did not eliminate the possibility that visitors who came into the house might be infected" (1984:80).

These women knew the importance of bearing witness to Jesus Christ. Christian service among Muslims begins with the act of bearing witness as well. Bearing witness is a simple task which can carry great impact. It is simple because it is something that any follower of Jesus can do in the power of the Holy Spirit. It takes no special expertise. It does not favor one gender—because both men and women can testify, and both men and women are eager to hear the message. And the center of attention is not the one bearing witness, but rather the One to whom witness is born.

And yet we find in the history of the church that the act of witness to Jesus can carry an impact all out of proportion to its apparent simplicity. John the Baptist prepared the way at the beginning of John's Gospel when he came as a witness to testify concerning the light. The Baptist himself was not the light, the Gospel makes clear: "he came only as a witness" (John 1:7, 8). John drew the attention of people to Jesus. He said, "I have seen and I testify that this is the Son of God" (v. 34). John was only a witness, and yet Jesus said that no human being was greater than John (Luke 7:28). The greatness of the Baptist came from bearing faithful witness to Jesus.

Since that first witness, many Christians have testified boldly concerning the light throughout the history of the church. These faithful ones encourage us to bear witness in the Muslim world as well. Christians who cross cultural lines to witness among Muslims must keep in mind the cultural setting and religious frame of reference. The Muslim world is not as welcoming to gospel witness as are some other cultural and religious groups. But, we find that at least one feature of the Islamic milieu invites Christians to bear witness openly.

Unschooled, Ordinary Christians

Jesus' final words on earth to his disciples, according to Acts 1:8, were that they would be *his witnesses*. Jesus said that the Holy Spirit would give the disciples power to do this task. He said the disciples would be his witnesses in hometown Jerusalem and also in an ever-widening circle "to the ends of the earth." Chalmer Faw, a former missionary to Nigeria under the Church of the Brethren, writes that this verse is the key text of the book of Acts. He notes that the three concentric circles of geography in Acts 1:8 correspond to the three major divisions of the Acts account (1993:30).

The work of the church is to bear witness to Jesus. This is not a witness to a religion or a culture or a set of doctrines or ideas, but rather to a person. And we see exactly what that meant when we follow the story of the first Christians in Acts. The first chance Peter had to speak to the people in Jerusalem, he immediately told of the life and death and resurrection of Jesus. "We are all witnesses of the fact" of Jesus' resurrection, he told the crowd on the day of Pentecost (Acts 2:32).

When Peter and John were later called before the religious leaders in Jerusalem, they were asked to account for their open witness. The Jewish leaders realized that Peter and John were "unschooled, ordinary men." The only qualification which they had—and the only authority by which they boldly preached—was that "these men had been with Jesus" (Acts 4:5-14). When they were threatened by the authorities not to speak in the name of Jesus, they left those threats in the hands of Jesus. They prayed together with the young Christian community for boldness to continue to bear witness. Since that time, unschooled, ordinary Christians of all ethnic and cultural backgrounds have served Jesus faithfully as his witnesses.

The Greek word translated "witness" in English Bibles is *martus*. This word came to mean both witness and martyr. The word points to a kind of Christian who is ready to die for the sake of the one to whom witness is born. Stephen is the first martyr mentioned in Acts, and James is the second. "The history of Christianity is filled with countless examples of believers paying the ultimate price for their beliefs" (Faw 1993:38).

Message of First Importance

The message which was at the center of the ministry of the first Christians—and the first missionaries—was the good news of Jesus Christ. It was a message which was readily identifiable. Paul gives the message in a "nutshell" in 1 Corinthians 15:3-8. He says that this is the one message which he and all the other apostles preach (v. 11). Paul lists the elements of this message as Jesus' death for the sins of humanity, his burial, his resurrection from the death on the third day, and his appearance to many witnesses after his resurrection. Paul calls these four elements of the gospel message "of first importance."

Paul gave the gospel message primary importance because he saw that this is what saved the Corinthian believers. Elsewhere he wrote that he is not ashamed of this message, because it is God's power (*dunamis*) for the salvation of everyone who believes it. As Paul went from town to town in Turkey, Greece, and Italy, he counted on this message to work in the lives of people of many different backgrounds to save them. He did not rely on words which are generally acknowledged to be wise, but rather he passed on the message of the cross (1 Cor. 1:17).

Paul was careful to make his witness in a manner which would match a message from above. He says that he did not want to empty the cross of Christ of its power by resorting to human technique and know-how. Instead, his aim was to highlight the power of God. He resisted the temptation to preach the gospel with eloquence or wise and persuasive words. Because the gospel is a spiritual message, and because it is "spiritually discerned," witness must be made in "words taught by the Spirit" (1 Cor. 2:13, 14).

The content of the gospel message, writes Church of Pakistan Bishop Arne Rudvin, is "handed over" to the evangelist. It is not the opinion of the messenger or a timeless human idea. "The main task of the twelve was to proclaim the *kerygma* or preaching about Christ. 'The apostle,' it has rightly been said, 'does not have any personal influence on the inner form of his commission'" (1976:382).

At the same time, there is also an element of personal experience in Christian witness. Peter and John said it was not possible for them to stop speaking about what they had "seen and heard" (Acts 4:20). Jesus' followers bear witness to his reality and resurrection power at work in the world today. We testify to what Jesus has done in our own lives. In some religions people will not claim that the founder of the religion is still alive. But Christians claim from the start that Jesus rose from the dead, that he lives today, and that he "is the same yesterday and today and forever" (Heb. 13:8).

Preachers of the Good News

Two friends named Hans Keescoper and Hans van Overdamme were sentenced to be executed together in Ghent in 1550. They were Mennonites, and their crime—which was judged to deserve the death penalty—was preaching the gospel. Before proceeding toward their execution, however, the two friends agreed together that on the scaffold Keescoper would take some time removing his stockings so that van Overdam could preach to the people gathered to watch them die. When the executioner offered to help Keescoper with his stockings, the first Hans said he'd do it by himself—so that van Overdam could speak a little longer. When Keescoper was finally ready, each Hans was placed at a stake and they "sacrificed their bodies to God" (van der Zijpp 1984:120-121).

One of the best-kept secrets of the Mennonite Church is that its founders were missionaries who went all around the world they knew bearing witness to Christ. Dutch pastor and professor Nanne van der Zijpp cites the above story as a typical example of how the early Anabaptists understood the importance of preaching the good news of Jesus. While most humans would be paralyzed with fear in anticipation of a painful death, the two disciples named Hans had the presence of mind to see the event as an opportunity to bear witness to Jesus Christ. This indicates an understanding of the importance of witness which can help us in the Muslim setting. "No temptation of rest or earthly well-being, no threat of torture of death could keep them from being preachers of the good news" (1984:120). The oldest Anabaptist congregation was a missionary congregation, states this professor.

Mennonites today have thus been given a special opportunity to understand the importance of witness, because it was central to the faith and life of the first Anabaptists. Almost 300 years before the great commission became important to the major Protestant denominations, Anabaptists were acting on it and taking the good news of Jesus Christ all around Europe.

> Whereas the Reformers no longer considered the great commission as binding, no biblical texts appear more frequently in the Anabaptist confessions of faith and court testimonies than the Matthean and Markan versions of the great commission, along with Psalm 24:1. They were among the first to make the commission mandatory for all believers. (Bosch 1991:246)

Public Opposition

An aspect of this story which has special relevance to witness in Muslim settings is that the early Anabaptists carried out their witness to Jesus in the face of strong public opposition. They were opposed by both the religious leaders and the political powers of their societies. In fact, the main source of information on the Anabaptists of the sixteenth century is the book recounting their deaths at the hands of European authorities, *Martyrs' Mirror*. Menno Simons dedicated his life to encouraging these persecuted believers to testify in the face of hardship. Menno Simons gave an insight into the motivation for this witness when he replied to someone who opposed him publicly:

> For since God, the merciful Father, has given us, poor creatures, the gift of his grace. . . . therefore it is that we would teach, proclaim, and impress on all men to the best of our ability, this revealed grace of His great love toward us in order that they may enjoy with us the same joy and renewal of spirit, and know and taste with all saints how sweet, how good, and how kind that Lord is to whom we have come.
>
> Therefore, we preach, as much as is possible, both by day and by night, in houses and in fields, in forests and wastes, hither and yon, at home or abroad, in prisons and in dungeons, in water and in fire, on the scaffold and on the wheel, before lords and princes, through mouth and pen, with possessions and blood, with life and death. (Wenger 1956:633)

The connection here to the Muslim context is that a convert to Christ under pressure from the Muslim community is in the same position which Menno was in. Menno was being hunted and persecuted solely for his witness. And yet he testifies to *joy*. We must believe that God also gives joy to the Muslim convert in a difficult situation. The gospel messenger should not hesitate to proclaim the good news of Jesus because she fears that a favorable response to the gospel will make life hard for the convert.

According to the Anabaptists, motivation for witness comes from the command of our Lord to make disciples of all people groups. On the other hand, Christians have a desire to see other people experience the same joy and renewal of spirit that they know. Their message is the love of God shown in Jesus Christ, and their motivation is also the love of God. They want others to taste the goodness of the Lord.

Crossing Major Boundaries

What happens when Christians cross major cultural and religious boundaries? Does the privilege of witness change? This is an important question for those considering the step of relating the good news of Jesus to Muslims. Two stories of early Christians recorded in Acts suggest a direction. The apostle Peter crossed a major boundary when he went to visit the home of Cornelius, a Roman military leader (Acts 10). In terms of ethnicity and culture, Peter the Jew acknowledged that he needed to change his mind about associating with Gentiles (v. 28). He learned that "God does not show favoritism" (v. 34; cf. 15:9), and that God accepted Gentiles in the same way that he accepted Jews (v. 35; cf. 15:8). In terms of religious background, we read that God heard the prayer of Cornelius and remembered his gifts to the poor (v. 31).

But the story does not end there. God's work in the hearts and minds of Peter and Cornelius was merely a promise of something greater to follow. That promise came to fulfillment through an act of gospel witness. God sent Peter to make human contact and to deliver the message Cornelius needed to hear. Peter went straight to the good news about Jesus (vv. 36-43). This was the message God commanded him to preach (vv. 33, 42). When the listeners heard the message, they received the gift of the Holy Spirit. Peter makes clear that his role in this cross-cultural, inter-religious encounter was to bear witness to Jesus (vv. 39, 41, 42). This carefully told story suggests that as Christian messengers pay close attention to cultural differences and religious backgrounds of non-Christians, the gospel message remains at the center.

Another story about crossing boundaries is Paul's visit to Athens in Acts 17. Paul's missionary travels in Greece challenged the apostle's cross-cultural creativity. In Athens, he took time to observe the local religious practices, which "distressed" him. When he had a chance to speak to the philosophers of Athens, Paul acknowledged the religious practices which he had observed, and used expressions of local poets to make intellectual contact. Then he went on to speak of the "ignorance" in the religion of his hearers (v. 30, cf. v. 23) and called for repentance. He wound up his address by preaching Christ risen from the dead and appointed to judge the world (v. 31). This story also affirms that in cross-cultural and inter-religious encounter, bearing witness to Jesus is an essential part of a sensitive approach.

One of Five Pillars

The act of bearing witness is well understood in Islam. One of the famous five pillars of Islam is the Confession of Faith or the *Shahaa-dah*—a word which comes from the Arabic verb "to bear witness (that)." And the verb has the same meanings as the Greek verb—to bear witness verbally and to die for the sake of that confession. A martyr in Islam is called a *shaheed*. In Islam Muslims must bear witness that "There is no god except Allah," and that "Muhammad is the apostle of Allah." In Muslim countries the witness to Allah and the Prophet of Islam is broadcast—each of the two parts repeated—in the call to prayer five times each day. It is one of the most common Arabic expressions on the tongues of Muslims, and in Muslim countries it appears in Arabic calligraphy almost everywhere. Repeating the Shahaadah with intention, Muslim leaders say, is all that is necessary to make a person a Muslim.

Thus in Islam bearing witness verbally is understood as normal—and virtuous—human behavior. Lamin Sanneh singles this out as a lesson Christians can learn from the experience of Muslim missionary work in Africa. Christian experience of Islamic *da'wa* (or appeal) "has shown Christians how seriously the vocation to witness needs to be taken" (1982:64). This special circumstance of the Muslim context invites Christians living among Muslims to bear witness to Jesus. Islam has done us a service. "The devotion and sense of self-sacrifice which Muslims have shown in obedience to the call to spread and establish the faith are a poignant reminder of what lies at the heart of Christian discipleship" (Sanneh 1982:64). Muslims may or may not agree with the object of gospel witness. Depending on the depth of the hearer's commitment to Islam, the witness to Jesus may confirm or contradict. But Muslims will find the Christian's *act of bearing witness* both familiar and favorable.

Clarify the Cross

Is there any reason to believe that the task of bearing witness to Jesus would not be needed in the Muslim world? The special circumstances of

Islam make this a worthwhile question to ask. Islam is the only major world religion which developed after the Christian faith. Muslims speak of a prophet called *'Isa* which they identify with Jesus. There is information in the Muslims' holy book, the Qur'an, about *'Isa*—some of which corresponds to what the New Testament says about Jesus. Is Islam perhaps a special case? Has it taken Jesus into account in a way which would make a gospel witness superfluous?

Early Muslims did take into account some of the biblical witness to Jesus when formulating their faith. But Islam has not generally affirmed biblical claims. Already in the third *surah* (chapter), the Qur'an begins to refer to Christian claims for Jesus and to give an alternate version— along with the challenge, "This verily is the true narrative" (3:62).

> In the years of its genesis, Islam, having originally taken a friendly attitude towards Christianity as the valid religion of revelation for the "nation" of the Christians, became antagonistic towards it by the mouth of its prophet, that is, virtually by the mouth of divine revelation. This antagonism to and indignant rejection of some cardinal elements of Christianity (Jesus' sonship, his death on the cross and consequently such doctrines as the Trinity, reconciliation, and atonement) are incorporated in the Qur'an, the basis of the Muslim faith, and so belong to the system of Islam. To reject Christianity is with Islam not merely the natural and intelligible reaction of every religion or world conception that has sufficient vigor in it to want to maintain itself; with Islam it belongs to its religious creed. (Kraemer 1938:354)

Though there is information about *'Isa* in the Qur'an, which amounts to about six pages in a book the size of the New Testament, most of this information is about his birth, and very little is about his life. Muslims do not have the "witness" to Jesus Christ which we find in the Gospels or in Paul's "nutshell" statement of the gospel. There is no good news about how God showed his great love by sending Jesus to die for the sins of the world. There is no message of forgiveness through the blood which Jesus shed. Since this good news is God's power for the salvation of everyone who believes, Muslims are still missing the witness which leads to their salvation.

In addition to supplying the essential information about Jesus missing from Islam, there is also a need to clarify the message of the cross from many misunderstandings created in the history of Muslim-Christian encounter. Mark Thomsen writes out of the experience of the Evangelical Lutheran Church in East Africa about how many Muslims live with the "burdensome past" of unchristian actions done in their territories by so-called Christian nations.

Muslims can easily come to the conclusion that these crusading or colonizing or warlike actions in their lands represent the Christian faith. And yet, writes Thomsen, not only have such actions *not* been molded by the mind of Christ, but they have often been a blatant denial and betrayal of the gospel. Christ calls Christians—especially those of European background—to confess as sin actions of the past which have been destructive and even vicious in relationships with Muslim peoples. Who will then set the gospel record straight? Do Christ's witnesses not also bear that responsibility? "Christian mission must be carried out among Muslim people in order that Jesus, vulnerable and *crucified*, might be known as God's power" (Thomsen 1996:196).

CHAPTER THREE

Conversion from Islam to Christ

"My name is Wanda. I am a Muslim."

The neighborhood women in the English class looked up in surprise at Wanda and then gazed at the teacher, Helen Nickel, to see how she would respond. The Canadian Mennonite Brethren missionary simply welcomed Wanda to the class, then silently said in her heart to Jesus, "This woman is yours, Lord. But I will not pressure her."

The two women became good friends through the class, in which the text was a simple English translation of the New Testament. Wanda brought with her a background of family trouble and spiritual searching. Helen prayed, and God worked in the heart of Wanda to draw her to Jesus Christ.

One day Wanda came walking directly into the house again as she had the first day and declared, "Helen, I want to be a Christian." Later she explained how understanding John 1:1 had opened a door for her. "When Helen led me to the Lord, I knew I didn't have to doubt anymore, and I was happy" (Burkholder 1984:144).

Wanda asked to be baptized, and she was incorporated into a local Muria (Mennonite) Church in Jakarta. Eventually many other members of her family became Christians as well. The church recognized Wanda's intellectual and speaking gifts and sent her around the Indonesian islands to encourage groups of Christian women.

Conversion is a reality in the lives of people. When people hear the good news of Jesus Christ and respond with faith, a real change takes place within their hearts. At the same time, conversion is a mystery because something happens which cannot be seen. Jesus said, "The wind blows wherever it pleases. You hear its sound, but you cannot tell where it comes from or where it is going. So it is with everyone born of the Spirit" (John 3:8). We cannot see the wind, but when the trees bend over from the wind's force, we accept their testimony that the wind is real.

This is how it is with people in whose lives God is working. They have a story to tell in which the reality of their conversion is unquestionable. And yet the variety and, often, the surprise of the ways in which people are led to Christ leaves us with a sense of awe. We need to listen carefully to the testimonies of people who have committed their lives to Christ to learn more about how God works and about how the gospel witness can line up with God's purposes.

Embarrassed by Conversion?

The Bible describes conversion with a variety of positive images such as new birth which portray the beauty and wonder of God's work in the lives of men and women. The founders of the Anabaptist movement rejoiced in the experience of conversion and used the biblical descriptions of it freely. Many Christians today feel the same.

Unfortunately, however, the idea of conversion has come to be viewed in a negative way by others, including some Christians. Lamin Sanneh, an African convert from Islam now teaching at Yale University, encountered this negative approach at age eighteen. When Lamin approached a Methodist church in Gambia to ask for baptism, indicating his conversion from Islam to Christianity, the British missionary at the church asked him to reconsider his decision!

Lamin found the minister to be uncomfortable with the idea of conversion; since that time he has found Christians in the West to be "very embarrassed about meeting converts from Asia or Africa." There are several reasons for this dislike of conversion, one which Lamin describes as the "guilt complex about missions" (1995:393). He might also have found a loss of confidence in the truth of the gospel. But this kind of discomfort about conversion was unknown to the early Christians, and the negative approach would have been unthinkable to the Anabaptists.

The negative approach seems to rest on three false assumptions about conversion. The first assumption is that conversion involves physical coercion or external inducement. The people taking the step, it is implied, are not really making a free choice. The second is that conversion is the work of human beings. The presupposition is that God does not work in the human heart. And the third assumption is that all change brought about within cultures is bad—that the *status quo* should be preserved at all costs (Martinson 1996:190). These assumptions need to be tested against the biblical concept of conversion and the way in which it takes place in peaceable gospel witness among Muslims.

Number Not Large

In the history of Christian mission in Muslim settings, the number of Muslims taking the step of conversion to Christ has not been large. Some of the finest gospel messengers have given decades of their lives to faithful ministry without seeing their Muslim friends decide to follow Christ. Experience in some regions of the world seems to affirm Kenneth Cragg's remark about Muslim converts, that "the source of amazement is not so much that there are few as that there are any" (1985:313). In recent years there have been reports of a more favorable response to the gospel in such places as Indonesia, Bangladesh, and sub-Saharan Africa. But in the Middle Eastern and North African Arabic heartland of Islam, response has remained tentative.

Some Christian workers become discouraged when the number of conversions among Muslims is much lower than in some other geographical and religious settings. Others wonder whether limited resources and personnel should be expended in areas of resistance or low response. But there are good reasons why the church does not grow rapidly in many Muslim contexts, writes David Shenk. "Some societies have developed formidable antigrowth propensities" (1983:151). One obstacle which prevents many Muslims from making a public commitment to Jesus—the Law of Apostasy—will be discussed in the next chapter.

In chapter one we noted that numerical success is not the basis for Christian motivation to serve Jesus among Muslims. Here we may also note that the presence of a very small "cluster of believers" is vitally needed even in situations where the church does not grow numerically (D. Shenk 1983:151). Fortunately, however, we have at our disposal many eloquent testimonies of Muslim women and men from many countries who have committed their lives to Christ. In these stories we find reasons to praise God for his work in the lives of people. We also learn what kinds of actions of Christians have made it easier for Muslims to choose Christ.

Free Response to the Word

The gospel is the power of God for the salvation of everyone who believes. When we preach the gospel, we can trust God to use that witness to work in the hearts of people. God's word is powerful, and we can expect it to accomplish the purpose for which he sends it. We know from Scripture what God's purpose is for the preaching of the gospel. God wants all people "to be saved and to come to a knowledge of the truth" (1 Tim. 2:4).

Paul saw a natural progression from the sending of the gospel messenger to the blessing of the convert. First the messenger tells the good news. The listener hears the gospel and responds to it with faith. Then the new believer calls on the name of Jesus (Rom. 10:12-15). Anyone who responds in this way, from whatever cultural or religious background, will not be disappointed. "For there is no difference between Jew and Gentile—the same Lord is Lord of all and richly blesses all who call on him." Paul knew the gracious intentions of God and anticipated a change of heart in those who heard the good news he preached.

The word "conversion" came into English via Latin from the New Testament Greek term *metanoia*, meaning a decisive turning in faith of heart and mind towards God. It is both a turning away, which is repentance, and a turning to, which is commitment to Jesus as Lord and Savior. Conversion is "an event that transpires within the depths of a person or community in response to God's movement within and upon the heart" (Martinson 1996:190). In the Christian understanding, conversion is the work of the Holy Spirit alone, working through the word of God (C. Shenk 1986:1). The heart responds spontaneously to the truth with faith.

Conversion is a miracle. It is the supernatural work of God in the life of a person. "If anyone is in Christ, there is a new creation; the old has gone, the new has come" (2 Cor. 5:17). The Old Testament gives an image for conversion in Ezekiel 36, where God says, "I will remove from you your heart of stone and give you a heart of flesh" (v. 26). Another picture is the dry bones in the valley which take on flesh and skin and come to life when God breathes into them (Ezek. 37). Only God can convert people. John writes that God works in the lives of people who receive Jesus by believing in his name. God gives them the right to become his children (John 1:12). He gives them a new birth.

The gospel messenger can bear witness to Christ, but cannot convert another person. The most that the gospel messenger can do is to invite another person to receive Jesus.

Realizing our total dependency upon God for his work in the lives of people reminds us to see clearly that no form of coercion or deception has a place in gospel witness. "Witness comes exposed, without the power to coerce. When coercion enters in, witness is perverted" (Martinson 1996:188). Conversion is a spiritual process, and physical methods are simply powerless to bring it about. Paul wrote that deception is also unthinkable for the gospel messenger: "We have renounced secret and shameful ways; we do not use deception, nor do we distort the word of God. On the contrary, by setting forth the truth plainly we commend ourselves to every man's conscience in the sight of God" (2 Cor. 4:2). The gospel messenger should do all she can in the inviting style of Jesus. But ultimately she must leave the conversion of another person in God's hands.

Spark of Spiritual Life

Do devoutly religious people need to be converted? This question often arises when westerners see the discipline which Muslims show in observing religious practices. It's not hard to admire the way in which Muslims fast during the month of Ramadan, or perform their prayers regularly, or memorize the Qur'an in Arabic. But outward expressions of piety do not necessarily correspond to the state of the heart. Jesus told us to expect this when he spoke about religious ritual and outward appearances in the Gospels. He taught, for example, that ceremonial washing does not touch the evil which comes "from within" (Mark 7:21). A few years ago a Pakistani columnist wondered about an apparent increase in the number of people who were performing prayers:

> Mosques have never been so crowded before. In private too, many more people observe the ritual sincerely, and not just to show off. But why is it there has been no corresponding increase in goodness, honesty, loyalty, compassion, tolerance and other virtues which prayers are supposed to back up? (Rahman 1990:11)

But there is a further reason why religious people need to be converted. Nicodemus, the man to whom Jesus said, "You must be born again," was a devout religious leader. We have no indication that Nicodemus showed any obvious moral flaw. Rather, we must assume that he showed a quality of piety and discipline in religious practice which would match the best of what we see in Islam. Nicodemus's need to be converted was not related to his apparent human goodness. Jesus said that if Nicodemus was to believe "heavenly things," it would require a spiritual rebirth.

Jesus continued his dialogue with religious leaders in the almost unbearably intense scenes of John 5–12. Here we find some of the strongest language in the Gospels. Why was Jesus so hard on religious leaders whose piety and discipline we would also want to admire today? What did he know that we don't? Was it that religious people too need the Holy Spirit to spark them to spiritual life?

Before his conversion, Paul was a Pharisee who was "faultless" in religious practice. His relentless persecution of Christians was a sign of his sincere religious zeal (Phil. 3:6). But he needed to be converted, and the dramatic story of that change is at the center of the church's understanding of the work of God in human lives.

Mennonites have had additional chances to consider the difference between religious stature and true spiritual life. Menno Simons left the testimony of his conversion. Menno Simons was ordained to the Roman Catholic priesthood in 1524, at age 28. His studies in Scripture led him to question a number of key Catholic teachings. He shared his knowledge of Scripture with his Witmarsum parish, but, he wrote, without spirituality or love: "I wasted that knowledge through the lusts of my youth in an impure, sensual, unprofitable life, without bearing fruit, and looked for nothing but gain, ease, the favour of people, splendour, name and fame" (Dyck 1995:46).

Menno Simons was a priest entrusted with the work of the church, growing in reputation, and yet he knew that his heart was not right with God. A change came in his life after he prayed earnestly and asked God to "create a clean heart" in him. He was then able to renounce his unchristian lifestyle and love of fame. Eventually he was able to open up his heart to a request to shepherd the scattered, persecuted Anabaptists.

After he left the priesthood in 1536, two of the first booklets Menno wrote were about conversion. He wrote "The Spiritual Resurrection" in 1536 and "The New Birth" in 1537. This was a significant theme in his subsequent ministry (Dyck 1995:42). But other early Anabaptist leaders—such as Dirk Philips and Hans Denck—wrote extensively on the new birth, conversion, and regeneration as well.

> *The new birth was the dynamic cause of early Anabaptism*, with the Scriptures as the formal root cause and the Holy Spirit as the enabling power. The initial experience of new life in Christ, individually and in community, was what made discipleship, the church, peace and all other emphases possible. New life and discipleship, for example, were interrelated and influenced each other. (Dyck 1995:52, italics Dyck's)

Menno Simons and other Anabaptist leaders were concerned with the conversion of people in Europe who called themselves Christians and who claimed to be part of the true church, and yet who showed by their lives that they had not come to life spiritually. Menno Simons does not hesitate to appeal to these Europeans—who had a respect for the Word of God and the opportunity to read it freely—to be born again. If the founders of evangelical Anabaptism consistently looked for conversion to take place in the lives of Europeans who considered themselves Christians and part of the true church, this encourages us to hope for the joy of conversion among Muslims who have not yet heard the good news of God's love for them in Jesus Christ or experienced God's regenerative work in their lives.

All Aspects of Personality

Is there any evidence that Christ attracts and satisfies the Muslim heart? asks Kenneth Cragg in *The Call of the Minaret*. The answer is yes, he says. "There is firm ground for the belief that many do and will reach out hands toward the Gospel, patiently and imaginatively presented, despite the antipathy toward it of much in the Muslim temper" (1985a:313). Part of the evidence is the testimonies of converts themselves. The following are just a few stories of the work of God in the lives of Muslims. Many other stories are available in such collections as *The True Path* (Mark Hanna), *Ten Muslims Meet Christ* (William Miller) and *Er zerbricht die Mauer: Mohammedaner finden Jesus* (Eduard Ostermann). These testimonies show God touching all aspects of human personality—what Cragg calls "the mind's understanding, the soul's expression, and the will's discipleship" (1980b:195).

Bedru Hussein grew up in a Muslim family in Ethiopia. He later became executive secretary of the Meserete Kristos Church, the Mennonite Church in Ethiopia. Bedru first came into contact with the gospel as a schoolboy when he picked up a piece of paper which the wind had blown across the schoolyard. It had on it a saying of Jesus from the Gospel. Later, in high school, he once saw a friend in the cafeteria with "an unusually bright face," he says. "I was in grade 12 and I had a great spiritual hunger, but there was no one to tell me."

The friend was a Pentecostal Christian who later invited Bedru to a youth center in Addis Ababa to see a film. Bedru accepted Jesus as his Savior that night, and later had the experience of being filled with the Holy Spirit. Everything changed for Bedru. "I started to love people—that was the change. And I knew Christ was in me" (Good 1994:12-13).

'Abd al-Masih grew up in a village south of Cairo and once found an Arabic Gospel of Matthew in the street. When he began to read it to friends, his teacher took the Gospel, tore it to pieces, and burned it. This made the boy think that to touch the Gospel was to be defiled. But some years later he heard a pastor reading from Matthew's Gospel in the house of a friend. He was attracted by the words and began a search which included trying to learn more about Islam. Finally he turned to Matthew's Gospel once more and found peace in the words, "Come to me all you who labor . . . and I will give you rest" (Matt. 11:28). 'Abd al-Masih suffered much persecution for his conversion, but he persevered and became a fervent and effective minister of Christ in the Middle East (Cragg 1985a:314-15).

Bilquis Sheikh, a Pakistani Muslim woman from a wealthy family, was especially drawn by the thought of God being like a father. Bilquis had enjoyed a good relationship with her own father and missed him greatly when he passed away. Once, Bilquis was recovering from an operation in a Christian hospital. She had gone through a period of considerable emotional distress. A Catholic nun suggested to her that she pray directly to God as to a kind father. This opened the door to her relationship with God (Sheikh 1978).

The Mind's Understanding

Another Pakistani Muslim, Muhammad Daud Rahbar, was also deeply impressed with his father's character. His father was a learned Muslim scholar in Lahore who had become a widower in his middle years. Daud saw how hard his father strove to be a loving double parent to his family despite the toll this took on the studies he loved. The son saw in his father a powerful example of self-giving affection and how much it can cost (Cragg 1980b:196). This led Daud to ask questions about the character of God. His testimony shows how deep the intellectual quest of some Muslim converts can be.

Daud believed as a Muslim that *Allaho-akbar* ("God is greater"). But he asked himself what divine greatness should mean in the area of compassion and suffering. "How was the infinitely estimable thing he found in his father to be related to the divine sovereignty? Could the same compassion and suffering be there also, appropriately infinite and ultimate?" (Cragg 1980b:196)

At Cambridge University Daud completed a doctoral dissertation on the ethical doctrine of the Qur'an which he published as *God of Justice*. He had no doubt that one of the attributes of God must be justice. But he asked himself what *truly divine justice* should mean. Daud compared various ideas of how the Creator God might act and was led to the thought that

God can be the Lord of Justice for men if He comes and lives with men and unambiguously suffers as they suffer. Else He is not the God of true and perfect justice. He must suffer at least as much as the worst human sufferer suffers if He is to be called Just. (Rahbar 1960b:5-6)

While dealing with these questions, Daud took a position at Ankara University in Turkey. In Ankara he came in contact with the gospel of the compassionate, suffering Christ. Actually, Christians did not attempt to persuade him to convert to Christ. But he experienced the intellectual integrity of Christian academic friends. He also began to read the New Testament. There he found, in the person of Jesus Christ,

a man who loved, who lived humbly like the poorest, who was perfectly innocent and sinless, who was tortured and humiliated in *literally the worst* manner, and who declared his continued transparent love for those who had inflicted the worst of injuries on him. (Rahbar 1960b:7, italics Rahbar's)

Daud found in the love of the suffering Christ what is truly worshipable. He found there the perfect divine justice and compassion he had been seeking. For him, the great Muslim obligation to "Let God be God" meant to see God in Christ reconciling the world to himself.

One Monday morning, Daud, his wife, and his two little girls went to the office of a chaplain named Meredith Smith and quietly said, "Sir, we would like to become Christians."

Smith was surprised to hear this from a devout Muslim who had been the Pakistani delegate to the World Conference on Islam. He asked, "What brought you to this decision?"

"After years of studying and teaching the great religions of the world," Daud answered, "we have concluded that Jesus is the way" (Khair-Ullah 1976:311).

Daud Rahbar's "Letter . . . to Christian and Muslim Friends," which he wrote in 1960, challenges his friends to face the questions which the Qur'an itself poses about the character of God and boldly concludes, "The Creator-God and Jesus are one and the same being."

This conclusion, of course, goes against the emphatic claims of Islamic doctrine as to the character of "Allah" and the humanity of "'Isa." Two of the key denials of the Qur'an are the divinity of Jesus and his death on the cross. When theological or religious systems forbid people to see God in Christ crucified, writes Cragg, then conversion is "necessary and right" (Cragg 1980b:197).

Creativity of the Spirit

Ironically, Daud Rahbar wrote just prior to his conversion that he expected conversions through reasoning alone to be very rare. Instead, he suggested that change of faith would be motivated "infinitely more frequently by love of charming virtues, of a magnetic person, or love for a group of lovable associates" (1958:50). Other Pakistani Christians like Frank S. Khair-Ullah and Michael Nazir-Ali, as well as former Irani bishop Hassan Dehqani-Tafti, agree that the love and kindness of Christian friends has been most attractive to Muslims. Siaka Traore of Burkina Faso and John Mahama of Ghana, both converts, testify that they came to Christ when Christians showed concern for them and valued them for who they were.

Other converts whom we came to know in Pakistan spoke of experiencing dreams or visions on their way to Christ (Nickel 1996b). Pat Cate, director of International Missions, has found something similar: "A large percentage of Muslim converts have had a dream in which Christ appeared to them and said something like, 'I am the way,' or, 'Follow me.' This has led them to find a Christian or a Bible, where they learned more about Jesus and put their faith in him" (1992:233).

When new believers out of Islam tell their stories, their conversion often appears to be the final link in a chain of experiences and encounters which can stretch back decades. Between the meaningful encounters may be periods of years which indicate little movement. Yet God the Father has been gently and steadily drawing them toward his Son.

Lamin Sanneh was attracted to the person of Christ after sensing the longing which Muslims have to venerate Muhammad as an intercessor between humankind and God. His conversion was not so much the rejection of Muhammad as a rejection of the Islamic orthodoxy which denies Muslims the hope they invest in the person of Muhammad. Lamin felt increasingly afflicted by the clash of Islamic authority with the inner reason of hope in a compassionate deity.

"The clearest expression of this Inner Reason is the gospel affirmation that although the 'Word' was God, 'it became flesh and dwelt among us, full of grace and truth'" (1984:173). Another African Muslim, Tokumboh Adeyemo, felt the contrast between Muhammad and Jesus. "All I remember of my moment of conversion is deciding to follow Jesus, the giver of life (John 10:10) rather than Muhammad and the way to God he brought" (1989:228). A revolutionary change for Adeyemo was understanding God in a personal way as his Father. He also realized that Jesus was more than a prophet. He came to accept Jesus as the sole

Mediator who offers access to God, and he began to read the Bible with new eyes.

Some Muslims seem to follow an intellectual route in which they carefully think through theology, while others appear to come at a spiritual level where God gives supernatural encouragement. God does indeed work in the hearts of Muslims, in spite of the many obstacles put up by Islam, and in spite of the weakness—and often sinfulness—of the gospel messenger.

CHAPTER FOUR

Making Disciples

Peter Zafar wanted to see his family again. Four years earlier, Zafar had made a decision to follow Christ. His wealthy business family in Lahore, Pakistan, had not been able to accept that choice. The family was known for its leadership in the Muslim community, and Zafar himself had been a Muslim teacher with a loyal following. So the family had pressured Zafar to reconsider, then had taken away his considerable inheritance. Zafar had moved to the coastal city of Karachi, where he had found nurture in the Christian faith.

But now some time had passed. Zafar was hoping his family would have come to terms with his conversion. He hoped that his family would receive him again as the eldest son despite their hatred for his faith.

When he returned home to Lahore, he learned his father had died. Nobody had bothered to inform him. Instead of the welcome for which he had hoped, his siblings abused him verbally for leaving Islam. Then they began physically to mishandle him. Finally his younger brother locked him up in a storeroom. Overnight the family would decide what to do with Zafar.

In the middle of the night, a servant who knew Zafar from earlier years took pity on him and unlocked the door of the storeroom. Zafar fled back to Karachi.

When people respond to Christ's gentle invitation to "Come to me," they enter a life of learning from their new Lord. Conversion is the "doorway to discipleship," as Henry Schmidt has so aptly expressed it. Discipleship for converts from Islam generally comes at a cost, such as that paid by Zafar. After conversion there is a lot of work ahead for both disciple and disciplemaker.

Every new Christian needs to find a fresh orientation according to the teachings and example of Christ. This is usually a challenge because

Christ's commandments go against the tendencies of human nature and the old and ingrained patterns of human cultures. When Christ speaks, he speaks from above, and his words are not easily obeyed by us who are from below. An extra difficulty with new Christians from Muslim background can be the need for a change of loyalties. For many Muslims the words and example of The Prophet of Islam—understood as the perfect human—may have held authority before their conversion. Now it is the Lord Jesus who gives the directions for living.

Making disciples in a Muslim context is one of the most exciting and fulfilling life involvements which any Christian can have. In this chapter we will discuss some ways in which the disciplemaker can be helpful to the new convert from Islam. We will also look at a special challenge to discipleship—the suffering which persecution brings.

Helping Young Converts

Jesus said that in addition to bearing witness to him, his followers would make disciples of all people groups. Making disciples would include baptizing those who receive Christ and teaching them to obey everything he had commanded (Matt. 28:19, 20). Jesus instructed his disciples to help new Christians through the first difficult stages of their new life into a developmental phase in which they could stand firm as disciples—and disciplemakers—in their own right. Of course, Jesus provided the model for disciplemaking by concentrating on twelve special followers during his three-year earthly ministry. We also have a helpful picture of disciplemaking in the story of Paul and Timothy. The same sort of caring attention to young Christians is needed in Muslim contexts as well.

Charles Marsh, a British missionary who served in North Africa for forty-five years, found that new converts from Muslim background have much the same needs as the new Christians in Acts who "devoted themselves to the apostles' teaching and to the fellowship, to the breaking of bread and to prayer" (2:42). Following a profession of faith in Christ, the disciplemaker should lead the convert in a period of individual instruction in all the fundamental truths of the New Testament. Reading Scripture together is essential, preferably in the colloquial language of the convert.

The disciplemaker, says Marsh, must explain how the aim is not to memorize long sections of Scripture for merit, as the former practice with the Qur'an may have been. Rather, the convert must see the Bible as God's instructions for how he should live as a Christian. Galatians is an ideal book for Muslim converts, Marsh found. The new convert must be able to explain his faith to others and to meet their objections from the New Testament (1975:88).

Under New Lordship

An area in which a disciplemaker can greatly help a young convert from Islam is to present Jesus as the new source of authority and as the example for daily behavior. Islam is a very full code of life, and it quite justifiably prides itself on having a law for every daily situation. The Islamic system of law or *Shari'ah* is directly related to the authority of the Prophet of Islam. The Qur'an puts the authority of the Prophet together with that of Allah in the frequent command, "Obey Allah and His apostle." But beyond the Qur'an is a great deal of material which aims to put forward the sayings and actions of the Prophet of Islam.

His sayings are contained in extensive collections of reports called the *Hadith*. Traditions about the behavior of the Prophet of Islam are called the *Sunnah*. Muslims view these sources as critically important. Sometimes they will describe the extra-Qur'anic sayings and actions of the Prophet of Islam as the "living Qur'an." "Orthodoxy upholds the primacy of the eternal Qur'an, but the masses have often been devoted to the created Logos, i.e., to Muhammad" (Nazir-Ali 1987:133). It is actually these traditions about the Prophet of Islam which fill out the impressive and comprehensive Islamic system of law for overseeing right conduct.

In "folk" or popular Islam, the role of the Prophet increases on a variable scale of veneration which extends to divinity. When Muslims venerate the Prophet of Islam highly, for example giving him powers of intercession and mediation with Allah, his authority over them becomes more than that of a teacher or prophet. They have pledged their loyalty to him and have in fact made him their Lord.

Disciplemakers can help new converts from Islam through a transfer of lordship. Donald Jacobs, a longtime missionary with the Mennonite Church in East Africa, found that in animist contexts the understanding of power sources is at the very center of the culture. When a person is converted to Jesus Christ, Jacobs asks, what happens at the level of the powers? "I am quite convinced that for a sustained conversion experience a person must elevate Jesus Christ to a position of Lordship in his power constellation and keep him there through Christ-honored living" (Jacobs 1980:136). Jacobs questions whether a commitment to Jesus Christ can last if Christ is thought of as simply equal in power to traditional powerful spirits and personalities. Jacobs suggests that Christian nurture must help a disciple realize that Jesus is above every other power.

This insight is helpful in Muslim contexts as well, perhaps especially in settings where animistic thinking is also deeply entrenched. The disciplemaker must present Jesus as the one to whom God the Father has given "all authority in heaven and on earth" (spiritual dimensions of this statement are discussed in chapter 10). In terms of disciplemaking, Jesus must replace the Prophet of Islam or any local *pir* or *sheikh* as the one who gives the rules for living. Out of his experiences in Muslim village in Sudan, Ken Peters writes, "Jesus Christ must become the great Sheikh of all Muslims, their spiritual guide, their intercessor, and the bestower of God's blessings" (1989:365).

Jesus needs to be Lord for the new Christian in a practical way. His words need to become the new commandments for living. Jesus asked people to listen to and practice his words. He said that people who do this build their lives on a solid foundation. Those who don't take Jesus' words to heart are headed for ruin (Matt. 7:24-27). God the Father drew the disciples' attention to the authority of Jesus at the time of the Transfiguration. "This is my Son, whom I love," he said so that the disciples could never forget. "Listen to him!" (Matt. 17:5). Then, when Jesus parted from his disciples at his Ascension, he said they would teach new followers to obey everything he had commanded.

Disciplemakers need to keep in mind that Muslims who become Christians may move from a highly structured life of rules into a life that seems to have little structure. Converts may experience a period of confusion. Does Christianity not spell out a way of living? After missionary David Shenk carefully described the Christian ideal for "Right Conduct" in *A Muslim and a Christian in Dialogue*, his Muslim colleague Badru Kateregga still said, "The Christian Church, unlike the Muslim Umma, has no system of universal law for right conduct" (Kateregga 1997:196).

This is a common Muslim charge. How do we respond? The New Testament does indeed contain a lot of practical teaching on Christian living—in the Gospels as well as in the letters of Paul, Peter, James, and John. Have some disciplemakers among Muslims tended to neglect this practical material because they want to make sure that the new believer understands her salvation to be based on grace through faith and not on works? The truth is that Jesus gave commandments to his disciples and instructed them to teach these to others as part of their disciplemaking. There is indeed a "law of Christ" (Gal. 6:2; cf. 1 Cor. 9:21). It would be a mistake to underestimate the attraction of Christ's teachings in the Muslim world.

Muslims often look on the teaching of Christ as a radical alternative to the Islamic system. (Whether they accept or reject such an alternative is quite another matter.) Of particular importance are Christ's teachings on revenge, adultery, divorce, prayer, and fasting, and on the relationship between exterior and interior religion. In these areas the contrast between the Islamic system and the gospel is most clearly seen (Nazir-Ali 1987:36).

Apostasy Brings Suffering

Do we have resources in the history of the church to help us with the challenges of discipleship and disciplemaking in a context where the convert is severely persecuted?

It is interesting to compare the dangers to Anabaptists in sixteenth-century Europe with the dangers to converts in Muslim contexts today. In sixteenth-century Europe, churches and governments dealt with the beliefs of the Anabaptists by torturing them into recanting. If they refused to recant, they were killed. Hundreds of such stories are recorded in *Martyrs Mirror*. In Islamic law, "there is unanimity that the male apostate must be put to death." Some schools of law allow the woman apostate to be imprisoned until she again adopts Islam, but most schools call for her death as well (Heffening 1993:635).

Though some modernist Muslims argue that this Law of Apostasy is not consistent with their faith (Rahman 1972), most ordinary Muslims believe their faith indeed prescribes the death penalty for leaving Islam. As the popular Muslim writer Maulana Maududi expresses it at the beginning of his book on the punishment of the apostate,

> To everyone acquainted with Islamic law it is no secret that according to Islam the punishment for a Muslim who turns to *kufr* (infidelity, blasphemy) is execution. Doubt about this matter first arose among Muslims during the final portion of the nineteenth century as a result of speculation. Otherwise, for the full twelve centuries before that time the total Muslim community remained unanimous about it. (Maudidi 1994:17)

Samuel Zwemer felt this was one explanation for the low number of conversions from Islam to Christ in the Middle East (1924). In any case, it puts the cost of discipleship for Muslims far higher than the cost for converts from many other backgrounds. And it explains why disciplemaking in this context will generally be more intensive than in other settings.

Some Christian workers from the West counsel that we must not look for a level of commitment which will bring the convert unnecessary suffering. It is true that outside workers must not insist on cultural changes not specified in Scripture. Also, outside workers must not require of converts suffering which they themselves are not willing to accept as well. But disciplemakers have no right to soft-peddle discipleship. They stand under the authority of the One who commanded them to make disciples.

Jesus told those who would follow him that they must take up their cross. He did not promise a life free of suffering—quite the contrary! The early Anabaptists accepted that their commitment to Christ would bring painful, and even deadly, consequences. Though they knew that adult baptism would bring them into conflict with the religious and political authorities of their society, they went ahead with baptism as a step of obedience and defended their action from Scripture with a commitment which confounded their interrogators. These stories of martyr witness from the past can shed light on modern discussions of what to look for in the lives of converts.

Cost of Disciplemaking

However, the Anabaptist heritage also contains instruction on the commitment of the disciplemaker. The step which the Anabaptist leader Menno Simons considered his conversion was the commitment to pastor the scattered and persecuted Anabaptists of Holland and northern Germany. His decision to encourage and instruct—to *disciple*—these hapless believers meant a readiness to die at any moment. Thereafter, the authorities were continually on his trail, and indeed there was a price on his head.

It is reported that some who showed hospitality to Menno were executed a short time after his departure—simply for hosting him. God kept Menno safe during his long and fruitful ministry, but as a disciplemaker he had put himself in the same danger that his flock was in. Is the disciplemaker among Muslim converts prepared to endure the same kind of suffering which the converts themselves suffer?

John Mahamah, a Muslim convert from Ghana who has pastored churches made up mostly of converts from Islam, says that the Muslim convert churches he knows which are strong and growing are the ones in which the leaders are willing to suffer along with the members.

In some settings, disciplemakers, especially those from developed countries, will have to struggle with various financial questions as well. When converts lose their normal ways of livelihood, they may need to rely more heavily on the disciplemaker for financial help or advice, or indeed for shelter or food. This is not an easy burden for the disciplemaker to bear.

Commitment to People

One of the most satisfying experiences of MBMS International ministry in Karachi, Pakistan, during the early 1990s was helping disciple a number of new Christians from Muslim background. Peter Zafar and Hashim Peter had come to Christ through the witness of other Christians, and they attended worship services at a Church of Pakistan congregation. But fellow worker Tim Bergdahl and I had the privilege of getting to know them well and helping them along in their faith. Both Zafar and Hashim (their respective birth names and thus used from this point forward) had suffered rejection by their families and communities when they committed themselves to Christ. Hashim had kept his family together even though his wife did not join him in coming to Christ.

On the other hand, many in the Pakistani Christian community treated these converts with suspicion. It seemed to me that the two men were not enjoying the level of fellowship they needed. One day Zafar said to me, "What I would like is to be part of a fellowship group in which we celebrate each other's birthdays." That comment struck me, and I made up my mind that with God's help I was going to create a fellowship group around Zafar.

We arranged to meet one evening each week at Zafar's small apartment. We sat on the floor for Bible study and prayer. An important part of our meeting was eating together. Eating together has a special significance in Eastern cultures. And the converts and other Christians in our group had sometimes experienced the insult of Muslims refusing to eat with them because they were Christians. Hashim was part of the group from the start. Other friends of Zafar, converts or Pakistani Christians with a love for Muslims, joined the group. Sometimes Muslims came to visit as well. The Bible study and prayer took on a special quality as we opened our lives to each other.

One member of the group was a German man who had come to Pakistan to smoke hashish and had become involved in Sufi Islam. Over time he had burned all his bridges. Now he wanted to rejoin his family in Germany and was looking for help from the church. Hartmut brought a lot of problems and a broken heart into the group, but the others embraced him in a remarkable way. Hashim would sometimes burst into tears as Hartmut was relating his woes.

Hashim's response to Spirit-led discipling was the most instructive for me. He would come to the meeting regularly and gladly but always with cares from trying to make a living in a difficult city. Almost every week he would bring a story of the cost he was paying at his workplace and in his family for his commitment to Christ, though he never complained. We would then eat together, study God's Word, tell our needs to each other, pray together, and sometimes sing worship songs.

At some point during the study, almost without fail, Hashim would let out a big sigh and say "Thank you, Jesus." You knew then that something from the Spirit of God had gotten through to encourage his heart. The same kind of encouragement does not come in a normal worship service. There needs to be deeper contact, a more intimate fellowship, to give converts strength to face their special challenges.

One of the creative activities we did together was to attend a Muslim meeting at a well-known mosque on a Thursday evening. The meeting was open to non-Muslims because this mosque was part of the missionary *Tablighi Jamaat* organization. Listening to the presentation and conversing with Muslim religious leaders later gave us a way of participating in an important part of Hashim's and Zafar's identity. It also gave us a way of making an open gospel witness in the hearing of the young believers.

A crisis came to our group when a popular Muslim magazine decided to print articles on the evangelistic work of our Church of Pakistan congregation. Both Hashim and Zafar were prominently featured in the coverage and labeled "apostates." The day after Hashim's photo was published in the magazine, he went to his teaching job as usual. The principal of the school said there was no alternative but to take Hashim's job away.

CHAPTER FIVE

Gathering Believers Together

Masood was attracted by the sound of singing. He walked toward the house from where the sound came and found a door wide open. Inside he saw about twenty men, women, and children singing a song about Jesus. One man sat in front of them, holding a book Masood recognized as the Bible.

Several people turned toward Masood and smiled. They beckoned him to come in, bending their fingers downward as people do in Pakistan. These Christians, from low-caste Hindu background, were despised by the Muslims of Masood's Ahmadi community of Rabwah. But Masood felt strangely comfortable among them.

After worship, the man with the Bible asked Masood to introduce himself. Somebody brought him a cup of sweet, milky tea. Sitting on the *charpai* (rope bed) beside the pastor, Masood asked how he could get a copy of the Bible. He asked why Christians believe that Jesus is the Son of God. The pastor gave him simple, gentle answers. The tea tasted good. This was Masood's first experience of the church (Masood 1986:44-46).

The church in Muslim contexts needs to be a new family for young converts from Islam. When Muslims become followers of Jesus, they become members of a worldwide multiethnic, transnational fellowship. Converts need the support of a community of believers who share their commitment to Jesus Christ. The challenge for Christian workers is to gather individual believers together for mutual support and accountability. The needs of Christian nurture in the Muslim context draw out all the best that the church now is—as well as what God wants it yet to be.

Hassan Dehqani-Tafti, former bishop of the Anglican Church in Iran and himself a convert from Islam, saw that no single disciplemaker alone is adequate to the challenge of nurturing new believers to maturity. His words have been a great encouragement to local church leaders in Muslim countries:

> No individual, however saintly, shows the love of God in Christ fully. Its interpretation needs the community of the faithful—the people of God. The church where two or three are gathered together in His name—this is the core of the matter. What a tremendous role is theirs, not least when their gathering together is in the midst of a world where for centuries Islam has prevailed. (1982:79-80)

Dehqani-Tafti and other national Christian leaders acknowledge that local churches in Muslim countries do not always fulfill their role in showing God's love to new Christians. But he represents a plea for a high view of the local church based on the scriptural portrait and on positive experiences of the church from the inside.

Much recent writing on the relationship of the church to Muslim ministry has attempted to apply the "homogeneous unit principle" to the Muslim context. The homogeneous unit principle suggests that Christians are most comfortable fellowshipping with 'their own kind,' and therefore that the church will grow most rapidly within ethnic or social strata. The orientation of some of this recent writing has been sociological and pragmatic, with the intention of maximizing church growth. Recommendations of what "works" in Muslim ministry are welcome. However, they must be evaluated according to the central teachings of Scripture on the church.

Two things are required if new Christians from Muslim background are to be gathered together in a helpful way. The church must provide the fellowship which the converts need. And at the same time, the converts must attach themselves to the church as their new family.

Community of the Faithful

New Christians from a Muslim background usually face rejection from family and community. As much as expatriate Christians would like to spare converts this pain by making it possible for them to live for Jesus in their home settings, converts are almost always rejected. It is not necessarily the case, as some writers suggest, that rejection should be blamed on Christian workers for extracting the converts from their settings or insisting that they abandon their culture. Converts face rejection for a number of reasons, among them a change of loyalty on the part of the convert and a feeling of shame on the part of the convert's family.

Being part of the *Umma* or Islamic world community means a proud political identity as well as a confident religious commitment. Leaving that community is understood as political treachery as well as religious apostasy. In most Muslim settings the community has a stronger hold on the individual than in modern Western societies. Committed Muslim families are understandably greatly disappointed when one of the children wants to leave Islam for a faith which is popularly understood as not only wrong but blasphemous. Even mildly committed Muslim families feel embarrassed by a child who takes a step strongly disapproved by the surrounding community.

When individuals confess loyalty to Christ and go against the beliefs and practices of their Muslim community, the pressure on them can be intense. Where can they turn for support? They need a new community, a new family. The church must help bear the social pressures the convert is experiencing. It is interesting to note that in the first centuries of the church this was one of the main functions of local churches. They bore the weight of persecution by political and religious authorities the early Christians were suffering (cf. Acts 4, 5). New Christians, treated poorly in home settings because of loyalty to Christ, received encouragement from their new community to stay true to Jesus. The church has borne this weight in other periods of church history as well, such as during the Anabaptist movement in sixteenth-century Europe. In many parts of the two-thirds world today the church is showing itself worthy of this role.

Mike Brislen, writing in an African Muslim setting, describes five needs of new believers from a Muslim background (1996:358-364). Converts need a church which provides them with security and rest in the midst of their anxiety-driven society and the added stresses which persecution brings. The church must also nurture a new sense of identity and worth in converts because society rejects their decision to follow Jesus. Converts need the church to help them, whenever possible, to maintain ties with their families. Converts also need healing and practical help and guidance through the Holy Spirit. Finally, the church can help converts by providing "solid, culturally relevant Bible teaching," along with a quality of worship which allows converts "to celebrate their new creation" (363).

Lone Ranger Christians?

The New Testament vision of the church is one in which people who come to Christ are "all baptized by one Spirit into one body" (1 Cor. 12:13). They come into a new multiethnic community with its offer of fellowship and its requirement of accountability. There is no concept in Scripture of an individual Christian going it on his own. Pakistani church leader Zafar Ismail expresses it well:

> Any idea of enjoying salvation or being a Christian in isolation is foreign to New Testament teaching. Individuals who, by the Spirit, and through faith, respond to the call of God in Christ, are intended by God to find and fulfill their vocation together in the church fellowship (1 Cor. 1:9; 1 John 1:3, 6, 7). (1983:385)

Converts, then, have responsibilities to the church. Michael Nazir-Ali, another Pakistani mission leader, counsels the disciplemaker to tell the convert why he is often met with suspicion by older Christians. The convert needs to be instructed in the ways of the local church. "Just as the local church must adapt itself to meet the needs of the Muslim convert or inquirer, so also the convert must make an effort to integrate into the local congregation" (1983:163).

Nazir-Ali prescribes a discipleship for converts which many Western missionaries may hesitate to require. He writes that converts need to learn to bear the suffering inflicted not only by family and former friends but also by Christians who misunderstand! Converts cannot really hope for anything better than what Jesus suffered from the people of God of his day, suggests Nazir-Ali. "Just as God vindicated Jesus openly before the Jews, so will he vindicate the convert before the Christians who view him with suspicion and hostility" (164).

High View of the Church

However, some foreign Christian workers, especially from North America, have not always held positive attitudes toward the church. They sometimes have little good to say about the church in their country of origin. Their attitude to local churches in the Muslim countries where they serve may be even worse. How can outside workers pass on a New Testament appreciation of the church to new Christians if they themselves are continually portraying the church in a negative way?

Christian workers in Muslim settings need an attitude toward the local church which reflects the positive view of Scripture. Paul was a missionary who knew of many serious problems in the local churches which he had planted. And yet he addresses these fellowships in the most affectionate terms (cf. 1 Cor. 1:2-9), and trusts that, despite problems, God will work through the church to bless the world.

> There is no other way but the church. When you read what St. Paul had to write to the Corinthians, you rather guess that their morals were not as pure as could be wanted. Again, when you read what he has to say to the Galatians, you know their conception of grace was about as faulty as it could be. And when you read the first few chapters of Revelation about the state of affairs in the churches named there—well, there you are. And yet it was just these churches that absorbed all new converts. (Christensen 1979:174)

Christian workers need to serve Jesus out of a high view of his Body. Converts from Islam need to experience the *koinonia* of Acts 2:42, "a sharing among Christian brothers and sisters, a sharing so intense that nothing was excluded" (Ismail 1983). Not all Western models of church have been helpful in nurturing this experience of fellowship. But Hans Kasdorf points out that the concept of a "believers' church" makes this possible. This theology of church, modeled by the early Anabaptists, saw the church as a voluntary and free gathering of believing members who have joined themselves together without any type of coercion for the purpose of carrying out the biblical mandate in the world. They serve each other as a "priesthood of all believers" and offer a broken world the ministry of reconciliation (1980:168-174).

The early Anabaptists, like the early church, experienced a need for mutual encouragement because of the persecution which was testing them all from without. Most converts in Muslim contexts experience a similar testing. Zafar Ismail recommends that local churches establish small "koinonia" groups whose members show a great interest and consideration for Muslim converts. Group members then bear one another's burdens and provide for the spiritual and material needs of the convert, according to Galatians 6:2. In this way, the convert's integration into the congregation is helped. Ismail concludes hopefully: "It requires no further comment that a convert led into 'koinonia' will definitely emerge as a living, stable Christian, a member of the body of Christ" (1983:392).

Role of Local Churches

Fortunately, recent years have brought some helpful encouragements to view the local church in a more complimentary way. Pat Cate, director of International Missions, sounds a positive note when he reports that he has found local Christians active in Muslim evangelism. "There's much we can learn from them. We should listen to them, work with them, have them speak in our weekly mission gatherings, monthly meetings, and annual conferences. We cannot take a know-it-all attitude; we need to come as learners" (1992:234).

Dean Gilliland also has a good word for the church. He writes that to focus narrowly on the conversion of individuals is not adequate. Missionaries need to recall the love for the church which characterized such apostles as W. H. Temple Gairdner. "Bishop Gairdner of Cairo truly believed that the church has the responsibility to be a body of patient and loving people among Muslims" (1997:11; cf. Cragg 1981:166, 167)).

The existence of ancient orthodox churches in Muslim contexts poses an important question to expatriate missions who want to work there. In many parts of the Middle East, for example, older churches are present which have been indigenous to the area for hundreds of years, some of them going back to the days of the early church. Other churches present before the arrival of a mission may have been planted in the last 200 years of missionary activity. What would it mean to enter and begin to work without giving any consideration to the local church?

Gabriel Habib has argued eloquently for evangelical missions from the outside to pay attention to the existence of the established local churches. General secretary of the Middle East Council of Churches, Habib asks evangelicals to recognize the ongoing renewal in Orthodox, Catholic, and Protestant churches in the region. He makes a case for a united Christian witness "in a region that perceives Christianity as heavily influenced and divided" (1990:257). Local Christians understand the importance of evangelism and mission, he says, but have difficulty with methods used by Western evangelicals "which are culturally and ecclesiologically inappropriate." Habib explains that local Christians look for a clear relationship between the missionary's home church and the local church where they seek to witness.

> We would ask all Western evangelicals who wish to come to our part of the world to proclaim the gospel to participate with the local churches in proclaiming this good news to those who do not know Christ, and thus be part of the witness that started at the time of Pentecost. (1990:260)

This question is perhaps especially relevant for mission efforts of the Anabaptist churches. Anabaptists can bring something distinctive into a setting where the experience of the "radical reformation" has not been known. At the same time they come with a high view of the church. There are several options open to them when they enter a new setting for mission where older or ancient churches already exist. One is to work in or through a church which is already active in the area. Another is to be part of a federation of Christian fellowships which work together on some things and present a united face to the country, and yet maintain individual identity. A third possibility is to work apart from the existing churches and to seek to plant a new church which has no ties to other churches.

Mennonite missionaries in the Middle East have generally opted not to plant Mennonite churches. Their vision has been to walk alongside and contribute to the existing church. They have felt that new faith communities should rise out of local vision and needs. LeRoy Friesen asserts, "The plethora of Western church entities both offending Eastern Christians and perplexing Moslems should not be exacerbated by yet another denomination" (Friesen 1992:64; cf. 22, 61).

The experience of Mennonite Brethren workers in Pakistan has been to work with and partly under the Church of Pakistan—a united church of Christians from mostly Hindu background who have come to Christian faith during the past 150 years. The partnership has included teaching at the Church of Pakistan seminary in Karachi, fellowshipping together in a local congregation, and suffering Muslim opposition together. At the same time the character of Anabaptist faith and witness has been appreciated. To talk about a Mennonite Brethren church of Pakistanis from Muslim background is premature. But if by God's grace such a church should come into being, why should it not take on the best transcultural characteristics of a believers' church?

Three Pakistani Churchmen

In recent years, Christian workers have been enriched by the writings of two-thirds world leaders on the church. These world writers sometimes see things differently from North American or European missiologists. Most recent Western writings on church growth, for example, are heavily oriented toward communication theory and anthropology, with a corresponding weakness in theological reflection (D. Shenk 1983:146).

Three Christian leaders from Pakistan have written in unison about the importance of the local church and have sometimes found themselves questioning influential missiological trends. All three are from Muslim background and have been active in the Church of Pakistan in the areas of evangelism and theological education. They have responded to Western missiological trends or principles out of their understanding of the church from Scripture and their experience of conversion from Islam to Christ.

1. *God works through the local church.* When mission thinkers made preparations to meet in Colorado Springs for the 1978 Consultation of Muslim Evangelism, most of the foundation papers related to cultural dynamics. Professor Charles Kraft had written in one of the key papers, "The development of more effective (and biblical) Christian witness to Muslims may demand that at least certain of the existing Christian communities in Muslim lands be bypassed." Frank S. Khair-Ullah challenged such assertions. As a result his paper on "The Role of Local Churches in God's Redemptive Plan for the Muslim World" was included in the consultation. Khair-Ullah's thesis was that the local church must *not* be bypassed. "In the final analysis," he wrote, "it is primarily through the Christians of the national church that their fellow-countrymen will be evangelized and formed into a strong local church in the country" (Khair-Ullah 1979:566).

Zafar Ismail wrote several years later that in Pakistan, a majority of national Christians and a great number of experienced missionaries prefer the approach of bringing converts into the fellowship of the local church (Ismail 1983:385). He advocated integrating the convert into the existing church, even though that is not an easy task. Both Ismail and Michael Nazir-Ali offer inside insight on why Christian communities in Muslim lands have difficulties in integrating converts (Nazir-Ali 1983:157).

2. *The local church needs renewal but also bears promise.* All three writers admit that local churches have serious problems welcoming and integrating converts. Khair-Ullah looks forward to renewal. "The Church can only play its role in God's redemptive plan if and when it has redeemed itself" (1979:569). Ismail finds that many in the church want to respond to the needs of Muslims: "The local church in Pakistan is quite concerned to make every possible adjustment to seek the favor and goodwill of the majority community around them" (1983:389). Nazir-Ali gives several good suggestions for how local churches can welcome converts from Islam. He writes that converts vitally need the "spiritual encouragement and nourishment" of the existing congregations (1983:163). To note that local churches have problems does not mean to lose hope that God can and does work through them.

3. *Western missiological theories must be evaluated by Scripture, indigenous experience, and a longer view of the church.* Khair-Ullah grapples with

the concept of "people movements" as introduced in a 1975 book by Pakistan missionaries Fred and Margaret Stock. Ismail examines the "Muslim church" approach advocated enthusiastically by "many of the Euroamerican missionaries and some of their national followers" (1983:385). Nazir-Ali questions whether there is biblical support for the "homogeneous unit principle."

Ismail argues—taking issue with a number of articles written in the West—that "the Christian minorities found in Pakistan are not ethnically and socially distinct from their Muslim neighbors in their respective localities" (1983:387). Nazir-Ali claims alternately that not all people like to become Christians in a particular homogeneous unit. "My own experience of Muslim enquirers and converts suggests that very few of them would have wanted to remain in their cultural milieu. Their questioning of its values is too radical for that" (1983:158).

But Nazir-Ali's main challenge to the homogeneous unit theory concerns its biblical base. "The existence of such churches seems to me . . . wholly against the testimony of Scripture and catholic tradition. . . . There is no mention whatever in early Christian writings of churches organized on homogeneous lines" (1983:160). Nazir-Ali allows for a "convert church" where no other Christian church exists. But even these "must recognize that they are part of the church catholic and be prepared to accept the authority and ministry of the wider Christian community" (1983:161).

These three churchmen are not against good ideas for reaching Muslims with the gospel. Each wants to be sensitive to "what the Spirit is saying to the churches." But Khair-Ullah suggests that some missiological thinking brought in from the West may be strongly driven by Western cultural values. He notes a preoccupation with technology in computer-aided research and statistics and finds that Euro-American missionary societies tend to be attracted above all by "tangible results" (1979:573-4).

4. *A more positive reading of previous efforts is possible.* Khair-Ullah has many good things to say about past missionaries among Muslims and the work of their converts (1979:571, see also 1975:819-820). Though the work of these missionaries may have resulted in few conversions, the missionaries were faithful and the quality of the converts was high. The achievements of the converts were out of proportion to their number. Khair-Ullah cites as an example the Muslim convert who wrote the Punjabi Psalter—the treasure of the Pakistani church. He gives a list of great servants from Muslim background which includes Imad-ud-Din and John Subhan (1979:576).

Khair-Ullah feels that the faithful work of the past has been up-staged by more recent missiological trends. A strict numerical measurement has belittled the ministry of many: "the excellent work done among Muslims was shelved, ignored and forgotten." He asks those who are preoccupied with numbers not to discourage evangelists "who have a burden to work among the seemingly unresponsive people" (1979:574).

Blessings of Reconciliation

Christians who are alive to the peace teaching of the New Testament will look with anticipation to see how the gospel blessing of *reconciliation* takes shape in a church which incorporates Muslim converts. Much of the writing on church planting in Muslim contexts in recent decades has advocated a "Muslim convert church" which missionaries keep separate from both the local church and the world body of Christ (Parshall 1985; Livingston 1993; Brown 1997). The arguments for keeping Christians separate are based on pragmatic considerations coming out of the homogeneous unit principle and on the experiences of converts who have not been readily accepted by local churches.

Whatever advantages this approach may have in terms of numerical growth, it forfeits the potential witness of the church as a community of reconciliation. One of the distinctive signs of the New Testament church is that former ethnic enemies become one in the body of Christ. Paul describes this reconciliation as one of the most astonishing blessings of the gospel:

> For [Christ] himself is our peace, who has made the two one and has destroyed the barrier, the dividing wall of hostility. . . . His purpose was to create in himself one new man out of the two, thus making peace, and in this one body to reconcile both of them to God through the cross, by which he put to death their hostility. (Eph. 2:14-16)

The ethnic distinctions which divided Jewish and Gentile Christians in the early church were even greater than the cultural differences between Muslim converts and local Christians in their neighborhoods. And yet Paul declares that Christ has demolished the dividing wall! When the church shows this reconciliation to the world, it bears witness to the power of the cross. "The existence of the new humanity is a magnificent demonstration of the shape the exalted Christ's power has taken in the world" (Penner 1990:57). Paul describes this coming together of Jew and Gentile in one body as a "mystery" (Eph. 3:6).

If Christ died to break down the walls between Jew and Gentile and all other ethnicities, Christian workers must question the impulse to build the walls again. That becomes all the more relevant in the Middle East, where ancient enmities persist and threaten the world with lingering conflict. "There is crying need in the Middle East today for communities of faith giving themselves to the *mysterion* vision and seeking to model the revolutionary acceptance, love and inclusion embodied by Jesus" (Friesen 1992:134).

Are mission agencies active in the region working to let the reconciling power of Christ be displayed? Strategies of separation may bring growth in numbers in the short term, but have we considered the impact on the church in the long term? If we neglect the peacemaking and wall-breaking work of Christ on the cross, could we not risk a great loss of credibility? "If we as brothers and sisters in Christ from around the world and from all levels of society cannot live the life of reconciliation and unity," asks Paul Hiebert, "what message have we for a world divided into hostile camps?" (1978:8).

Is it possible that missiological trends and theories can sometimes come to command such loyalty that it becomes difficult to challenge them? Mission workers agree that God wants the church to grow among Islam. All want to see larger numbers of Muslims come to Christ. But can missionaries hope to build with good materials on a solid foundation if they neglect the biblical teaching on the church in the interests of what Phil Parshall calls "a rather extensive strain of pragmatism?" (1985:190).

After a lifetime working among Muslim Pathans in the North West Frontier Province of Pakistan, Danish missionary Jens Christensen wrote some straightforward advice on "the Muslim convert in the Church." Like all of the chapters of *The Practical Approach to Muslims,* Christensen's words on gathering believers together will strike many readers as provocative. His strongest challenge is not to the local church or to the Muslim convert, but rather to the disciplemaker who passes on to the convert an attitude toward the church:

> If the Muslim convert is ever going to be a living, stable Christian, a member of the body of Christ, you have need of an entirely different kind of faith. You need to believe that the church on the spot, despite all its failings, is the body of Christ, and given fair teaching and guidance it will function as the body of Christ. Then you need to believe that it is your bounden duty to turn your raw recruit over to that church. He must know why, of course, but having been told why, if he still refuses, you can do nothing more for him. (1979:174)

These words go against the grain of much evangelical writing on ministry to Muslims in the past three decades. Christensen's approach is typical of the classic missionaries of the early 1900s who went to the Muslim world with a thorough grounding in both biblical theology and Islamic studies, who knew the scriptural languages and local vernaculars well, and who shared a deep commitment to the church of Christ and to the apostolate to Islam. Christensen concluded with a little quip for those of us who are still not convinced: "Finally, you have to have faith to believe that even if the Church fails once, twice or a dozen times, in the end, its failures will not be so many or so dismal or so disappointing as the failures of missionaries throughout the years" (1979:174-5).

CHAPTER SIX

Conversation with Muslims

Getting to know people of other faiths means coming into daily discourse with many fascinating individuals and families. These friends may believe and act quite differently from the ways we believe and act. A challenge for many Christians is to learn to get along with people who do not share their faith and practices. Christians in many parts of the world have lived for centuries as minorities among other dominant religions, including Islam. These Christians have much to teach Western Christians with less experience living in multiethnic and multifaith neighborhoods. They can help us learn to respect people who have different cultural and religious practices while remaining true to our faith in Jesus Christ.

Two essentials of Christian behavior among people of other faiths are friendly personal contact and meaningful conversation. We need to listen carefully to people of other faiths and hear what they say, even as we maintain freedom to confess our own faith. Believers who carry on nothing beyond a monologue appear to lack humility. Witness must not be a one-way street.

The friendly conversation we seek has sometimes been called dialogue. But this term has come to represent a variety of meanings and as a result tends to create confusion in discussions about ministry to Muslims. Some define dialogue as "simply a matter of sharing, getting to know one another, and gaining a new understanding of the respective faiths" (C. Shenk 1986:4). This sense of dialogue is essential to our relationships with people of other faiths. We must get beyond what Calvin Shenk calls "library versions" of other religions to be authentically present with people and to get to know them as persons (1992:7). A second definition of dialogue is a faith conversation in which participants are free to confess their deepest beliefs and even to attempt to persuade each other of their truth. This seems to be the way the word is used in the New Testament.

A third concept of dialogue seems to reflect the philosophical assumptions of religious pluralism. This view asks Christians to enter each interfaith encounter without presuppositions of truth and without anticipating where the discussion will lead. This concept encourages Christians to expect that some new truth may emerge from outside of the faiths of both participants. This is often put forward as the only approach which can allow people of different faiths to live together peaceably.

Peaceable gospel witness among Muslims requires a genuine respect for the people we live among along with a firm commitment to the truth of the gospel. Entering the conversation with relativistic assumptions is not helpful, first of all, because it does not suit the Muslim mindset and its comfort with claims of absolute truth. Second, it is not realistic to the actual human meetings between Muslims and Christians. Third, the relativist approach is not the way to pursue peaceable relationships between religious communities. Lamin Sanneh suggests that denial of personal faith commitments is counterproductive. "We should not delude ourselves into thinking that we can speak to others only if we give up what we believe, for denying one religion, even our own, does not increase religious tolerance" (1996:8).

Out of his intimate experience of the African setting, Sanneh writes that an open acknowledgment of differences is the best point from which to build peaceful coexistence. "Christianity and Islam are united perhaps less by the things they have in common than by what divides them" (1996:7). He explains that genuine differences in faith safeguard the identity of believers, and that "genuine identity promotes pluralism as well as mutual trust" (1996:7).

InterServe director James Tebbe echoes this theme. He finds that a confident Christian faith helps healthy relationships with Muslims. Integrity in Christians' relationships with Muslims requires that we work from a clear theological position and points to the need not to hide our true thoughts. Christians should know where they stand, and they should be prepared to give account for their beliefs in friendly relationships. "As we are confident of a firm ground on which to stand, we will be able to draw close to Muslims without fear. In our theological understanding we can find clear confidence. Absolute truth is vital to us" (1996:174).

Conversation with Muslims must include a respect for our friends which allows us to listen to them carefully and to consider seriously what they say about their faith. It must also include a good knowledge of our own faith and a loyalty to the Savior we confess.

Not Uncertain Questioning

What can we learn from the stories of interfaith contact and the use of the vocabulary of dialogue in Scripture? The book of Acts recounts the experiences of the first Christian missionaries among Samaritans, Romans, and Greeks as well as among Jews.

The New Testament uses three Greek words which contain the root from which we get our English word *dialogue*. Martin Goldsmith, whose experience among Muslims has been in southeast Asia, gives a helpful explanation of these words.

Two of the words, which Luke uses in his Gospel, imply considerable questioning and uncertainty of thought. Paul uses these same words with the negative sense of "uncertain questioning which he sees as an expression of empty futility" (1982:120).

The third word, which Luke uses in Acts, "avoids any suggestion that the apostles were wracked with uncertainty or questionings as they engaged in mission." In Acts 17 this third word, which the NIV translates "reasoning with," is used alongside "proclaiming" (v. 3) and "preaching the good news about Jesus and the resurrection" (v. 18). "Throughout the Book of Acts Luke uses the word dialogue with this sense of convinced preaching, but the apostolic proclamation is often dialogue in the sense that it is not mere monologue" (1982:120). An example of this is in Acts 24, where Paul presents the faith in the context of a conversation with Felix.

Goldsmith concludes from the biblical use of the word that true Christian dialogue will include aiming to convince Muslims of the truth of the gospel. Such dialogue will arise out of the hope that Muslims may be converted to faith in Jesus Christ. But dialogue will also include listening "to the heartfelt needs and deepest thoughts of our Muslim friends" (1982:121).

The account of Paul's visit to Athens gives an example of a missionary carefully considering the frame of reference of his audience to express his message in an understandable way (Acts 17:16-34). Some have used this story to advocate a style of dialogue which is tentative about gospel witness. Michael Nazir-Ali suggests that this would be to misunderstand the text. Paul certainly shows his listeners the respect of taking what they believe seriously. However, this is not the only lesson of the account.

> If this is a model for interfaith dialogue, then unequivocal procla-
> mation must follow positive evaluation—even at the risk of jeop-
> ardizing the dialogue. Paul is patient in the face of unbelief and even
> ridicule; he is sympathetic to the spiritual aspirations of his listeners
> and aware of their religious tradition. These attitudes in dialogue
> deserve commendation. Paul is clear in his presentation of the ap-
> ostolic preaching of the death and resurrection of Jesus Christ, and
> this, too, deserves commendation and imitation. (1987:119)

Confident Christology Essential

Serving Jesus among Muslims requires a strong faith in Jesus within the terms through which the New Testament bears witness to him. Islamic faith challenges some of the central Christian confessions about Jesus (cf. Kraemer 1938:354). In daily life in Muslim settings, faith and religious practices come up much more frequently as topics of conversation than in many Western societies. Ordinary Muslims will deny biblical affirmations with assurance and finality. A Christian worker in a Muslim setting who does not have Christology straight will likely soon become confused and discouraged.

Our commitment to the basic elements of Christian faith, such as the Lordship of Jesus and God's revelation of his divine self in Christ, will determine the quality of our conversation with Muslims. Peter Hamm was one of a number of missiologists and biblical scholars in the Anabaptist tradition who have encouraged a confident Christology. A mission leader in the Mennonite Brethren Church, Hamm wrote that Christians in contact with people of other faiths must "discover anew the centrality of the person and message of Christ. This is the *kerygma*" (1967:244).

We must have a firm grasp on the coherent center of New Testament teaching, the proclamation of Jesus crucified and risen from the dead. Victor Adrian, another MB mission leader, highlights the unique mission of Jesus to reveal God to all of humanity. "He alone has intimate understanding of the Father's mind and will. He alone can make the Father known" (1994:37).

Calvin Shenk notes that Peter's confession, "You are the Messiah, the Son of the living God" (Matt. 16:16), was made in a context of considerable religious sophistication. The opinion of some people that he was a prophet did not elicit Jesus' recommendation. "Human categories, even the highest human categories, are inadequate to describe Jesus" (1992:2). David Shenk draws attention to the subsequent Transfiguration where God himself declared from heaven that Jesus is his Son (Matt. 17:5). "He wanted the disciples to get the core of the gospel clear. Jesus is not one among others. Jesus is the one and only Savior and Lord" (1994:137).

George Brunk III, another Mennonite scholar, examines the exclusive claims which the New Testament makes for Jesus and which Jesus made for himself. He concludes, "God's *conclusive* revelation and action in Jesus the Christ gives to this One an *exclusive* dimension of truth which, because of its universal relevance, is *inclusive* of all humanity" (1994:52, italics Brunk's). John E. Toews writes after a study of key texts that "the confession that 'Jesus Christ is Lord of all' is the central theological claim of the New Testament writings" (1996:7).

The conviction that Jesus is Lord carries implications for our encounters with people of other faiths. "Jesus is Lord" means that everything and everybody rightly belongs to him. Our motivation for mission is thus to bring all of humankind to acknowledge Jesus as Lord, "because he owns us all, and has a just claim on us all" (Rudvin 1976:377).

Gospel witness is not merely saying that Jesus gives us saving knowledge, or that Jesus reveals something from God. Our message, rather, is that in Jesus Christ, himself, God is revealed. "For the apostolate to Islam it is quite clear that this is the crucial point. The Lordship of Jesus in the absolute sense is contested by Islam and thereby the very foundation and motive for Christian mission to Islam is questioned" (Rudvin 1976:377). Rudvin suggests that to translate the stature of Jesus into the Islamic context we should use the expression which Muslims use for Allah, *Rabb al-'Aalameen*—"Lord of the worlds."

This is essentially the conclusion which Islamics scholar Daud Rahbar reached after a study of Qur'anic and biblical theology. He worded his Christology in a rather striking way: "If the innocent Jesus, who forgave and loved His crucifiers from the Cross, was not the Creator-God Himself, then the Creator-God is proven to be inferior to Jesus. And this cannot be. . . . The Creator-God and Jesus are one and the same Being" (1960b:8). Later, after his conversion, Rahbar wrote that this high Christology was the best basis for fruitful dialogue. "It is when I spent several weeks comparing the characters of Jesus and [the Qur'anic] Allah and came to know the superiority of Jesus over Allah that my heart melted and I sought to touch the feet of the crucified Lord" (1960a:6).

Listening and Confessing

The style of dialogue which best suits the gospel of peace is also ready to hear the partner in the conversation. James wrote: "Everyone should be quick to listen, slow to speak and slow to become angry" (James 1:19). Christian workers among Muslims must express their own faith in a peaceable manner and listen with respect and interest to the expression of the other.

One of the finest written examples of this kind of dialogue grew out of the experience of a Mennonite missionary in East Africa. David Shenk, serving under Eastern Mennonite Missions, and Badru Kateregga, a Muslim, worked together in the Department of Philosophy and Religious Studies at Kenyatta University College. The two professors taught comparative religion in a team-teaching relationship which often meant a witness from one faith to another in front of their students. They experienced how the hearing and the giving of authentic witness can bring pain, because the issues reach to the basic questions of the human situation.

But they both felt that witness in dialogue is essential. "We need to learn to speak with one another from within our respective communities of faith" (Kateregga 1997:18). In *A Muslim and A Christian in Dialogue*, each author sets out his faith in twelve chapters on topics such as "The Seal of the Prophets," "The Mission of the Umma," and "Salvation." They show that it is possible for Muslims and Christians to converse without slipping into polemic on the one hand or denying their respective faith commitments on the other.

What is it that makes a conversation between people of different faiths possible? A first and crucial condition is this: respect for our partners in the conversation. Roelf Kuitse writes that the first step in loving our neighbor is to take seriously the neighbor's "thinking, acting, and way of believing and expressing faith" (1981:4). That means getting to know the religious tradition of Islam, writes Kuitse, but it also means meeting people in the midst of how they experience life and their religious tradition. It involves listening carefully to what people say about their faith, answering their questions, and being ready to be challenged by their faith.

The basis of our respect is realization that we share the same humanity. The partner in the conversation is "a fellow-man with the same fundamental needs, aspirations and frustrations, whose religious experience and insight are as worthwhile as the missionary's, simply because he is a living human being" (Kraemer 1938:356).

The second condition of conversation is a love that imitates the love of God for the world. God showed his great love in the suffering and death of Christ on the cross. "This mysterious love enables us to reach out to our Muslim neighbor following Jesus' pattern of humility and service" (Hoover 1994:1). That love encourages us to continue the conversation even if the partner loses motivation.

A third condition is the trust that God will do his own work in the midst of the conversation. "Witness can . . . be dialogic in style, because it realizes its human need to listen and learn with respect for fellow human seekers, being confident that the monologic address of the divine call comes authentically from God alone" (Brunk 1994:52). We can relax and listen because it is not we who will persuade and must therefore do the monologue, but rather it is God alone who can speak in a way to call people to himself.

Modesty and Faithfulness

Confessing Jesus as Lord, however peaceably, is not considered appropriate by some people. They say that making exclusive claims for one's faith in a world of many faith commitments shows arrogance and intolerance. They counsel that when Christians dialogue with people of other faiths, they leave truth claims to one side and enter the conversation without presuppositions.

It is true that Christians, just like people of all other faith commitments or none, may be arrogant in their estimate of themselves or their regard of others. In biblical terms this arrogance is a sin which needs to be confessed and renounced. But is this sin integral to the act of bearing witness to Jesus?

When we accept the truth of the gospel and pass on its good news, we are not merely sharing our own opinions or experiences. We are not making up "cleverly invented stories" (2 Pet. 1:16) to display our philosophical skill. We are also not saying that we know we are right and all others are wrong. This is outside the scope of our human capacities. Rather, we have made a faith commitment to Jesus, and in the terms of that commitment, the blessings of God come to people through the proclamation of the gospel.

Paradoxically enough, the universal blessings of the gospel come through an exclusive revelation. God loved the world (universal) so much that he gave his one and only Son (exclusive), in order that whoever (universal) believes in him (exclusive) may not die but will instead gain eternal life.

The claim to an exclusive revelation may offend people in a relativistic culture. But in gospel terms, the love of the Father is given through the Son. God himself has given the following testimony about his Son: "God has given us eternal life, and this life is in his Son. He who has the Son has life; he who does not have the Son of God does not have life" (1 John 5:11, 12; cf. John 3:36). If the Christian wants the love of God, and rich blessings such as eternal life, to reach the non-Christian, she has no option except to proclaim the good news of Jesus Christ.

In determining the need for modesty, it is helpful to distinguish messenger from message. The gospel messenger is limited in understanding. He or she may have much human weakness to confess. "Our fallenness and finitude demands modesty and humility. Our convictions must be expressed with respect and reverence" (C. Shenk 1986:4). We need to guard against taking ourselves too seriously. And we must not speak with others as if we were superior.

The gospel message, however, is something else. The gospel we proclaim is not a matter of our own opinion. We have no right to act as if the gospel is on the same level as myriad other faith statements. It is a message which we receive by grace and pass on as of first importance. "We are not in a position to surrender that which is not ours," notes Calvin Shenk (1986:4). It is our responsibility to be loyal to our Lord and faithful to the gospel.

A missionary scholar who has articulated this distinction while living in the midst of Islam is Church of Pakistan Bishop Arne Rudvin:

> Everyone with some knowledge and experience of the piety and the expression of religious experience in non-Christian religions, in our case Islam, will of course admit that they are subjectively as good as anything in Christian piety and experience, and we as Christians must respect them as much (or as little) as we respect our own piety and experience. Some of us, indeed, may doubt if our own piety and experience as such is really worth sharing, but while it may be very right to be modest in this regard, the evangelist, as herald, is not called to be modest on behalf of his Lord or on behalf of the Gospel. (1976:383)

Christians who claim we must speak tentatively about our own faith in conversation with Muslims to avoid arrogance and intolerance raise another important question. Our Lord has said that we will be his witnesses; he has commanded us to make disciples for him; he has made many exclusive claims about himself which have come to us through the Scriptures, including "I am the Way, the Truth, and the Life" (John 14:6).

The first Christians acted on all of this in a straightforward manner and prayed to the Lord for help to "speak your word with great boldness" (Acts 4:29). They knew the personal challenge of the Lord: "If anyone is ashamed of me and my words, the Son of man will be ashamed of him when he comes in his glory and in the glory of the Father and of the holy angels" (Luke 9:26). When modern Christians decide not to speak of their faith with confidence, out of regard for the reigning religious pluralism of Western culture, don't they risk the possibility of disobedience or disloyalty to their Lord?

Missionary statesman Lesslie Newbigin deals at length with the accusation of arrogance in *The Gospel in a Pluralist Society*. He finds that this accusation arises out of an uncritical acceptance of the "plausibility structures" of modern Western culture. If making absolute claims for Jesus is characterized as being arrogant, Newbigin asks, what about the claim to be able to relativize all absolute claims?

> There is an appearance of humility in the protestation that the truth is much greater than any one of us can grasp, but if this is used to invalidate all claims to discern the truth it is in fact an arrogant claim to a kind of knowledge which is superior to the knowledge which is available to fallible human beings. (1989:170)

Gospel witness does not mean speaking about personal religious ideas or religious experiences. Rather, it is a witness to the facts of history. As Newbigin said on another occasion, to withhold these remarkable facts puts in question our love and respect for people of other faiths.

> If, in fact, it is true that almighty God, creator and sustainer of all that exists in heaven or on earth, has—at a known time and place in human history—so humbled himself as to become part of our sinful humanity and to suffer and die a shameful death to take away our sin and to rise from the dead as the first-fruit of a new creation; if this is a fact, then to affirm it is not arrogance. To remain quiet about it is treason to our fellow human beings. (1988:328)

Truth Claims Welcome

Christians should enter dialogue with Muslims with a confident faith in the gospel, a loyalty to Jesus, and a respect for the partners in the conversation. It is also helpful to be realistic as to how conversation ordinarily takes place in Muslim-Christian encounters. Most Muslims are comfortable with truth claims. Muslims may not accept the biblical witness to Jesus, but they are at home in thought patterns which have a place for absolute truth. And they do not share the philosophical pre-suppositions of religious pluralism which have captured Western culture:

> Generally the Muslim will reject the basic principles of dialogue. He does not agree that Christ is present in Islam nor that Islam and Christianity are both partial truths. The Muslim is confident that he has a message from God which he must deliver to those who have not yet submitted to the will of God. (Goldsmith 1982:119)

Thus it happens that in some modern encounters, Muslims speak confidently about their faith while Christian representatives are only willing to speak tentatively. Muslims also do not hesitate in dialogue to deny the central affirmations of Christian faith. A striking example of this is the collection of papers read at the November 1974 Symposium of Christian and Muslim scholars organized by Oratio Dominica and published later in English as *We Believe in One God*. The very first paper of the collection, written by a Muslim scholar from Vienna, begins with a closed door: "If theology is discourse about God, then Islamic theology makes no assertions concerning Jesus Christ. Islam rules out any incursion of the human into the sphere of the divine. . . . In Islam Jesus has a thoroughly human dimension." After explaining how this is so, the scholar concludes, "Despite the respect, therefore, which Muslims show towards Jesus as a messenger sent by God, no practical results are likely to come from Muslim-Christian dialogue in regard to Christ" (Balic 1979:1, 7).

Michael Nazir-Ali suggests that such a conversation would be typical and explains why this is so:

> A Muslim scarcely ever has much hesitation in affirming what he believes to be the truth and in trying to persuade others that it is indeed the truth. He understands this to be part of the Islamic *da'wa* (or appeal) to the outside world, and will do all that he can to see that it is effective. (1983:148)

Nazir-Ali acknowledges the value of Christians and Muslims sharing their faith with each other. However, he finds the reluctance of a Christian to persuade the other partner of the truth of the Christian faith "an utterly unnatural posture." Goldsmith adds to this that dialogue coming out of a confident Christian faith would be respected by the committed Muslim. "He may well despise the lack of sure faith implied by a form of dialogue which does not seek to convince and convert him" (1982:120-121).

Most of the conversation between Christians and Muslims, however, takes place not in formally organized meetings but rather on the
day-to-day level. Two friends, one a Christian and the other a Muslim,
exchange information about each other's beliefs and customs in an in-
formal setting. Or Christians and Muslims live together in the same
neighborhood and have to face common problems. This daily conversation provides many opportunities for Christians to show love in practical ways. That is the topic of our next chapter.

CHAPTER SEVEN

Lives of Love

As the train rolled along, a missionary spoke to his Muslim fellow traveler about Christ. Mr. Nassim listened with an open heart. The missionary was intrigued and asked Mr. Nassim why he seemed so ready to listen to the gospel message.

"Years ago," replied Mr. Nassim with deep emotion, "a Muslim friend and I saw two Catholic sisters holding out their hands to receive money for a new hospital building. As we passed them, my friend, instead of giving some money, spit into the extended palm of the sister.

"Thoughtfully, the sister pulled out her handkerchief and wiped off the spit. Then, smiling at my friend, she said, 'All right, that was for me. Now what will you give Jesus?'"

Mr. Nassim looked at the missionary with tears in his eyes and to the click of the train on the track said, "Can anyone forget love like that?" (Abdol Massih 1979:86).

Expressions of love and acts of kindness are greatly appreciated all over the world, not least in regions of high Muslim population. Christian service is worthwhile in itself and need not be justified by reports of spiritual results. There is sufficient motivation in the nature of God and in the teaching and example of Jesus. At the same time, acts of kindness are attractive to people and inevitably raise the question of motivation. When Christians are questioned about their motivation for service, they should be prepared to bear witness to Jesus and his love. And when they do confess their faith, they need to be careful to live a life worthy of the gospel, consistent with the Lord they confess, so that they don't give people reason to refuse the message.

Christian service is an important part of ministry to Muslims. Arne Rudvin defines Christian service as "to live out the Gospel in selfless service and social action for others who are in need and trouble"

(1976:379). The best definition, however, may be the commandment of Paul: "Live a life of love, just as Christ loved us and gave himself up for us as a fragrant offering and sacrifice to God" (Eph. 5:2).

Acts of Kindness

Christians strive for a lifestyle of love simply because Jesus has shown us that this is the way to be fully human. Jesus came healing the sick. He came concerned with human suffering. He felt compassion for people in need and acted out his compassion in practical and helpful ways. "Compassion for its own sufficient reason, response for need's own sake—these were the hallmarks of Jesus' ministry, whether with hungry crowds or private sufferers" (Cragg 1985b:141). Christians follow in Jesus' footsteps when they do the same. Jesus' greatest display of love was giving his life for the world. "Greater love has no one than this, that he lay down his life for his friends" (John 15:13). That's the example of Jesus, John says simply, then adds, "And *we* ought to lay down our lives for our brothers" (1 John 3:16).

When Jesus told the story of the Good Samaritan, he highlighted the importance of simple acts of kindness. The Samaritan traveler saw a case of obvious human need and responded in the appropriate way. This parable is an unforgettable illustration of what it means to "Love your neighbor as yourself" (Luke 10:27). The neighbor, Jesus stresses, includes the person who is different from us in ethnic and religious background. Indeed, the neighbor includes the one we may consider our enemy.

God loves all people, and Christians are called to be the channel of his unconditional love for the world. Jesus makes the behavior of God the standard for the behavior of his followers: "Be merciful, just as your Father is merciful" (Luke 6:36). Acts of kindness do not require a positive response to be justified. We love other people because God loved us first (1 John 4:7, 8, 11, 12, 20, 21).

Rudvin calls Christian service or *diakonia* "the true fruit of the preaching of the Gospel about him who gave himself for us and who came to serve rather than to be served" (1976:380). The very essence of God on which his divinity rests is *agape* (the Greek word for "love" in 1 John 4:8-10). "From this it follows that the purpose and meaning of the life of the Church is to live in his love and to try to live it out in service in the Church and outside" (Rudvin 1976:381). When Christians follow the compulsion of Christ's love (2 Cor. 5:17), they are set free from self-centeredness and enabled to serve those who are in need of service.

"Following Jesus into the disciplines of the kingdom has given the church gifts of ministry" to share with Muslims, writes Dean Gilliland. Sometimes Christians work as if a polemical approach is needed, when instead the witness calls for an intentional meeting of needs, for visible acts of mercy, and for demonstrations of divine power. "When Christians show holistic concern, verbal witness about Jesus will be credible and will create a reconciling atmosphere for dialogue" (Gilliland 1997:11).

Response to Human Need

The needs of people give us a second compelling motivation for Christian service. Both John and James write that the needs of others are sufficient reason: "If anyone has material possessions and sees his brother in need but has no pity on him, how can the love of God be in him? Dear children, let us not love with words or tongue, but with actions and in truth" (1 John 3:17, 18). "Suppose a brother or sister is without clothes and daily food. If one of you says to him, 'Go, I wish you well; keep warm and well fed,' but does nothing about his physical needs, what good is it?" (James 2:15, 16).

Rudvin encourages Christians to keep their thinking clear so that they do not end up using compassionate ministries in a way that seems to influence Muslims inappropriately. "Our only motive in *diakonia* should be, as an expression of love, to assist the needy person because he is in need" (1976:380). Institutions such as hospitals and schools, which Christians have established in response to human need, should not become instruments of manipulation. This degrades medical, educational, and Christian service in general. It is also a sign to Muslims that Christians lack faith in the Word of God and in the power of his Spirit.

"Muslims have been willing to acknowledge and accept acts of impartial Christian love and charity," writes Roy Hange (1994:23). He recounts examples from the growing treasury of positive experiences of Mennonite Central Committee workers in Muslim contexts. The story of Bob and Jill Burkholder shows how Christians, by the power of the Holy Spirit, can be peacemakers in violent settings. The Burkholders worked in war-torn southern Lebanon to build up relationships of trust between themselves and the Muslims, Christians, and Druze they worked with. In August 1985 Bob was kidnapped and taken secretly to a building where he was interrogated.

Hange writes, "The first question was, 'Are you afraid?' Bob replied in Arabic, 'I fear no one but God.' This answer broke the ice with his

Muslim interrogators and the following two hours was more a discussion of MCC's work in Lebanon than an interrogation. Their final words to Bob were 'keep up the good work'" (1996:71).

When Bob arrived home fourteen hours after his capture, he was greeted by a living room full of religious leaders of various Muslim and Christian groups who were fighting each other at the time! "Their common concern for Bob, who had shown sacrificial concern and love for them, was revealed to be greater than the barriers and bitter divisions between them" (1996:71).

Christians who work to serve the needs of Muslims create space for reconciliation and peaceful faith conversation. John and Elizabeth Shirk served in a Muslim village in Nigeria under MCC in the 1970s. One day they were called to help a young nomadic Fulani woman and her prematurely born child. The Shirks provided immediate shelter for the woman and 11 members of the extended family who were travelling with her. The woman was expecting her two-pound child to die, but Elizabeth helped to nurse the child by feeding it milk with a medicine dropper until it was able to drink milk from its mother. Six weeks later, the child had gained three pounds and was healthy enough for the family to continue their journey.

Some months earlier, the Nigerian State Ministry of Education had wanted to caution the Shirks against inviting Muslim students to join them in their home for weekly Bible studies. The parents of the students had reported these activities of the Shirks to the Ministry, and there was a chance that the couple would be deported. However, the impact of their helping to restore the fragile life of the infant far overshadowed the opposition to Bible studies. "Deportation no longer was a threat, and the credibility and testimony of the MCC workers were strengthened. Much more, God was honored, and His love was made known" (Thiessen 1995:32).

Shining Like Stars

There is a third important motivation for Christian service. The lives Christians live must be consistent with the good news message at the heart of their faith. Will Muslims listen to a message which is somehow contradicted by the life of the messenger? Iranian bishop Dehqani-Tafti found that message and life must match:

> Words alone cannot bring the Muslim to the foot of the cross. . . .
> Christians must show in their lives how Christianity is in truth the

incarnation of the love of God. Most of the Muslims I know who have followed Christ have done so because of the sacrificial life and sustained love of some Christian friend. You cannot bring the Muslim to Christ unless you love him personally. (1982:79)

The gospel message is a precious treasure with which Christians have been entrusted. Being able to hold out this message to others is a great privilege. Christians must not dishonor this treasure by bringing shame on it in the way they live. That is why Paul encouraged the Christians in Philippi to conduct themselves "in a manner worthy of the gospel of Christ" (Phil. 1:27). "Christians who have heard the gospel and embraced the good news of redemption must be constantly concerned that this wonderful gospel is not brought into disrepute through their unseemly behavior" (Ewert 1995:46). Paul wrote further that Christians should be blameless and pure, without fault, "shining like stars in your lifestyle, as you hold out the word of life" (Phil. 2:15, 16).

The apostle Peter wrote to Christians who were suffering persecution for their faith that they should always be ready to give a reason for the hope they had. But he urged them to be circumspect in their behavior and to keep a clear conscience, "so that those who speak maliciously against your good behavior in Christ may be ashamed of their slander" (1 Pet. 3:16).

When Words Are Restricted

In a number of Muslim countries, Christians are not free to speak openly of their faith to Muslims. All verbal expression of the gospel is understood as proselytization and even prohibited by law. In situations where Christians are restricted in what they can say, acts of love and compassion give them a way to express their faith.

The history of the church in Muslim countries includes many stories of people who have sacrificed their lives doing deeds of love in situations where an open witness to Christ was difficult or impossible. One of the most encouraging contemporary stories is the Christian service of Herb and Ruth Friesen. Herb and Ruth have spent several decades offering practical help in a situation where Muslims have been fighting among themselves. The Mennonite Brethren couple from Kansas began a ministry of eye medicine in Kabul, Afghanistan, in 1969. Serving with the International Assistance Mission (IAM), Herb and Ruth helped lay the organizational and legal groundwork for a national eye care delivery system called NOOR. They served with IAM until 1979 in the midst of great political upheaval. During that time the NOOR Institute developed into a top-flight care center and school of eye medicine. Herb has chronicled those exciting years in his book *A Reluctant Surgeon.*

In 1982 the couple moved to Pakistan, into which millions of Afghan refugees were pouring following the 1979 Soviet invasion of Afghanistan. Herb worked at the Christian hospital in Taxila and then took over leadership of the Afghan Eye Hospital in Peshawar. Ruth began her "gate ministry": counseling, consoling, assisting, and witnessing to a steady stream of refugees who crowded around the gate of the Friesen's home daily. "Only eternity will reveal the fruits of this ministry of compassion—and often total exhaustion," says Herb (Hardaway 1996:13). By working on eyes injured in the Afghan conflict, often to reconstruct a face together with other surgeons, Herb became a world authority on eye injuries from war.

When the door to Afghanistan opened again after the retreat of the Soviets, the Friesens moved to Mazar in northern Afghanistan to start the Mazar Ophthalmic Centre in 1994. Again under IAM, the Friesens and their colleagues treated 20,000 to 25,000 patients a year and organized a medical training program to upgrade the skills of the six doctors and six nurses on staff. Then in 1996, with the MOC in good hands and running well, the Friesens journeyed to Gilgit in northern Pakistan to help start a vision center. The Friesens have worked in settings where their help is greatly needed and deeply appreciated. As people they are respected and loved by Muslims. But bearing witness to Christ can bring very real danger.

Richard and Ann Penner are another couple who were willing to serve in Afghanistan amid danger. The Winnipeg couple and their three children were sent by MBMS International in 1978 to take managerial duties with IAM in Kabul. Even after two coworkers were murdered in 1981, they returned to Kabul to serve during the Soviet occupation. They remained in Kabul during the 1980s when many others fled because of the guerrilla war. Through this faithfulness they earned great respect from the local people. Early in their assignment, Richard described the gentle, patient approach required in a setting where words are restricted. "We become friends with those we work with, try to understand their needs, try to get together with them—which is difficult—and then we are able to discuss with them" (Burkholder 1981:21).

Because of the political and religious dynamics, the Afghanistan work shows few visible spiritual results. But that's not to say that the acts of kindness are without value, or that the witness is going unheard, or that God is not working in the hearts of people. "The presence, life, prayer, ministry, witness and invitation of the redeemed cluster who meet in Jesus' name is vitally needed even in situations where the church does not grow numerically," writes David Shenk. Some societies have developed "formidable antigrowth propensities." But that is not a reason to terminate Christian presence or deny compassionate ministry. "In those situations it seems the Holy Spirit is especially concerned about maintaining an authentic presence and witness" (1983:151).

Signs of Divine Glory

In some Muslim countries, missionaries are accused of using hospitals, schools, and other compassionate ministries as unfair means to convert Muslims. Some Muslim leaders say there is no Muslim consent for Christians to do their *diaconia* there (Rudvin 1976:389). What is the appropriate response to accusations of proselytization? It is true that many—likely most—missionaries hope that kindnesses done in Jesus' name will draw attention to Jesus. Those who work in such ministries often want to see Muslims come to Christ. Does this mean that they are using compassionate ministries in an unfair or deceptive manner? The answer is at least partly influenced by the Muslim context.

Christian acts of kindness have the potential to point beyond the physical world to a loving God. Jesus himself made this link explicit in the Sermon on the Mount when he commanded, "Let your light shine before men, that they may see your good deeds and praise your Father in heaven" (Matt. 5:16). Compassionate ministries may also have the privileged role of encouraging a response to God. Christians serve humanity with the ultimate hope that God will be glorified. "If anyone serves, he should do it with the strength God provides, so that in all things God may be praised through Jesus Christ. To him be the glory and power for ever and ever. Amen" (1 Pet. 4:11).

An interesting circumstance of Christian service among Muslims is that Muslims are familiar with some of the acts of compassion of Jesus from the Qur'an. The Qur'an tells how 'Isa "healed those born blind and the lepers," and "brought the dead to life once more" (3:49; 5:110). But the wording of these verses is intriguing. Though the miracles are acknowledged, the glory associated with them is not allowed to attach to Jesus. These verses specify that Jesus was only able to do these things "by [Allah's] leave" (The phrase appears four times in 5:110). This verse and its exegetical tradition seem to have studiously avoided letting the miracles of 'Isa point to his divine glory.

Could this be one of those places in gospel-Islam encounter where an apparent point of contact turns out to be a potential disconnection?

Kenneth Cragg explains how in the Gospel of John, "the deeds of Jesus, in healing and teaching, are disclosures, or manifestations, of glory and truth" (1985b:247). Jesus' miracles of healing and meeting physical need are signs of a greater reality (sign or *ayat* is another Qur'anic concept), according to the Gospel of John. They are related to an apprehension of Christ himself. John shows that such miracles as the feeding of the five thousand—though described in other Gospels as responses of compassion for people and their physical needs (Matt. 14:14; Mark 6:34; cf. Matt. 15:32; Mark 8:2)—point beyond material sustenance to the Bread of Life whom people need even more urgently than they need physical bread.

Jesus felt compassion for people when he saw their physical hunger. He acted and met that need. But he also saw that the people would eat that food and still die (John 6:49, 58). Then he indicated the source of satisfaction of the deepest human needs. "Here is the bread that comes down from heaven, which a man may eat and not die. I am the living bread that came down from heaven. If anyone eats of this bread, he will live forever. This bread is my flesh, which I will give for the life of the world" (John 6:50, 51). John records that in the aftermath of such personal claims of Jesus, even some of his disciples "turned back and no longer followed him" (6:66). People took offense.

There is, therefore, a strong gospel connection between acts of kindness done in Jesus' name and witness to Jesus himself. Compassionate ministries can attract attention to the One full of compassion (James 5:11). But Christian service must never degenerate into a means to induce or manipulate a wanted response. Christians in Muslim settings must have a clear understanding that they do acts of kindness because they are followers of Jesus and because there is a great human need for these ministries. "We serve because God is love" (D. Shenk 1983:150).

Prepare Hearts for the Gospel

Muslims themselves will quickly recognize whether our Christian service flows from hearts of love or from dishonest or selfish motives. Asian and African Christians have much to teach us here. African converts from Islam frequently testify that they were attracted by the transparent love and friendship of Christians and by being valued for just who they were. F. S. Khair-Ullah observes, "unless by the grace of God we touch another heart with love, it may never really come to know the much greater and wonderful love of God for him" (1975:824).

Lebanese leader Fouad Accad tells the story of an African Christian woman who befriended her Muslim neighbors. By the time Accad came to visit the family, their hearts were already prepared to hear the gospel. Accad has found that a Muslim who has been taught that Christianity is a heresy probably won't listen to a presentation of the gospel, "unless that Christian who is in contact with him has become a close, dear friend to him and has a character that commands respect" (1997:31).

David Shenk tells of how Christian missions worked in Somalia between 1945 and 1960 to develop quality medical, educational, and development programs. Soon after Somalia's independence in 1960 it became illegal to propagate any religion except Islam. Yet the humanitarian work of Christian agencies, including the Somalia Mennonite Mission, had developed an image for the Christian faith which provided room in the society for the emergence of unobtrusive Christian fellowships. "Muslims frequently ask about the meaning of Christian mission presence. Such occasions open opportunities to express the faith in us, with the gentleness and respect missionary Peter had counseled in biblical times (1 Pet. 3:15-16)" (1994:197).

"Keep Up the Good Work"

There are many compelling reasons for Christians to live lives of love among Muslims. Acts of kindness give Christians a way to express God's compassion for humanity and to meet urgent physical needs. They also provide fitting opportunities to bear witness to Jesus and his love. Christians have tended to err in two directions. One error has been to preach the gospel without responding to the immediate human needs in front of them. The second error has been for the church to be so focused on improving the situation of humanity that it forgets the heart of its message. "The real Gospel is not development or progress but the proclamation that He loved us first," reminds Rudvin. "We only attain real life through faith in the crucified and risen Lord" (1976:382). Christian acts of kindness cannot themselves create faith or give people new life, "for it is the pure Word of God who alone is able to create faith" (1976:380).

We need to continue to work at a biblical balance of word, deed, and presence. Mennonite mission agencies, like many other Christian groups, have struggled to strike a balance in Muslim settings (Friesen 1992:115-119). We are tempted by the extremes of a "spiritualized gospel" and a "materialized gospel," notes LeRoy Friesen—because each, in its own way, is less costly to share. Perhaps the Muslim context, with its special sensibilities and its unique theological understandings, can draw out a more authentic integration.

Roy Hange finds an encouraging lesson in the story of Bob and Jill Burkholder. He reflects on Bob's remarkable release by his Lebanese kidnappers and notes the words with which the captors sent Bob home:

> If there is a way forward for Christians with Islam, it may be for Christians to "keep up the good work" in acts of love in Muslim contexts, to encourage each other on the way of service in our respective faiths, and to find contexts where day-to-day dialogue can build understanding as Christians commend Christ as the One through whom God has made us infinitely free to love, free to understand Muslims on their own terms, and free to forgive. (1994:23)

CHAPTER EIGHT

A Cross and a Dove

Harold Vogelaar, a Middle East missionary with the Reformed Church in America, once saw a striking painting by a Egyptian Muslim artist named Muhammad.

Muhammad had painted a portrait of a powerful young man. The man held a sword in one hand and a dove in the other. Vogelaar asked Muhammad what the painting meant. The artist replied that the dashing figure symbolized Islam—which always came offering peace but, if it was not accepted, carried a sword to impose Allah's will on society. Vogelaar asked Muhammad whether he had ever considered painting a man who held the dove of peace with two hands.

Muhammad thought for a long time and then replied, "I would have to paint a portrait of Jesus" (Thomsen 1996:196).

Vogelaar's conversation points to an important fact about gospel witness among Muslims. There are aspects to the gospel message which especially come to life in the context of Islam. The New Testament calls the Christian message the "gospel of peace." This peace dimension is portrayed as a crucial part of the "song" we sing when we tell the good news of Jesus. In fact, the peace "notes" are characterized as an extremely attractive part of the song. In the history of Christian mission, has there been some hesitancy to include the peace dimension in the gospel message? Can the song be complete, can it make its full attraction felt, if it is not the gospel of peace? This chapter celebrates the gospel of peace and the following one attempts to show how the nature of the gospel should affect our manner of gospel witness.

There are many good reasons why the peace emphasis must be a part of our gospel witness among Muslims. Among them is the long shadow of a campaign of violence against Muslims initiated by the leaders of the medieval church and carried out by fighters who considered themselves Christians. Europeans fought and killed Muslims under the banner of the cross—the symbol of God's unconditional love. They created resentment among Muslims which continues until today and left in their wake deep misunderstandings about the nature of the Christian faith. The gospel must be reclaimed from these misunderstandings.

Another reason for a peace emphasis is the striking contrast which appears when we put the authors of the Christian and Muslim faiths alongside each other. When we compare the stories of Muhammad and Jesus and compare the Scriptures associated with those two figures, issues of peace and nonresistance come into the spotlight.

> The military dimensions of original Islam and its uninhibited embrace of the political are certainly crucial factors in deterring the Christian from a positive response to Muhammad. For they are so sharply, and in some apologists, so confidently alien to New Testament criteria, as to seem to warrant unreserved rejection by any thinking that has even remotely understood Gethsemane. (Cragg 1984:31)

Muslims themselves notice these contrasts, and Christian workers of all backgrounds serving among Muslims tend to give them greater significance. These contrasts in turn point to crucial differences in how God is understood in the two faiths.

A third reason to sing the notes of peace is that violence is one of the most urgent contemporary challenges in our world. Reports of violence in Muslim contexts come to us in a steady stream. And the 1991 Persian Gulf War presented the striking phenomenon of Western Christians approving, and even participating in, the killing of Iraqi Muslims. "Christians and Muslims are being forced to think together on this extremely difficult but essential topic because our common human future depends on it" (Thomsen 1993:125).

Peace at the Heart of the Gospel

In the first recorded encounter of Jesus' disciples across cultural and religious boundaries, Peter calls the gospel "the good news of peace through Jesus Christ, who is Lord of all" (Acts 10:36). Paul also calls the Christian message the "gospel of peace" in his list of spiritual weapons in Ephesians 6 (v. 15). It appears Paul took the gospel of peace from the Isaiah text he quotes in Romans 10:15. The messengers in Isaiah 52:7 "bring good news" and "proclaim peace." They come with a message of comfort and salvation which makes people burst into songs of joy. Their message of peace is so attractive that even their feet are made beautiful!

At the heart of the gospel is a story of peacemaking. The good news is that the divisions between people, and between people and God, have been done away with through the death of Jesus on the cross. Paul writes, "For [Christ] himself is our peace, who has made [Jew and Gentile] one and has destroyed the barrier, the dividing wall of hostility" (Eph. 2:14). God reconciled all things to himself by making peace through the blood of Christ, "shed on the cross" (Col. 1:20). The New Testament locates the point of reconciliation for people of diverse ethnic backgrounds and religious communities at the cross of Christ.

This means that whenever we proclaim the gospel with integrity, we proclaim peace as well. We tell people that because of the faithfulness of Jesus, "we have peace with God" through him (Rom. 5:1). The Christian message is one of reconciliation (2 Cor. 5:19). We tell people that God has made them his friends, and that through Christ he doesn't hold their sins against them but rather offers forgiveness. The ministry which God has given us is to plead with people on Christ's behalf: "be reconciled to God" (v. 20).

The death of Jesus on the cross also breaks down the walls between people. The New Testament stresses that even the high wall between Jew and Gentile has been demolished. "Reconciliation with God," writes Mennonite mission leader Stanley Green, "always assumed and declared to be coextensive with reconciliation to one's fellow humanity, is inextricably at the very core of the gospel message" (1990:24).

Jesus gave a special blessing to people who make peace (Matt. 5:9). He taught his disciples to love their enemies and pray for those who persecute them (5:44). Muslims are often intrigued by Jesus' teaching to turn the other check toward someone who has struck you on the right cheek. "Do not resist an evil person," Jesus taught (5:39). The disciples had the opportunity to see Jesus live out his own instructions. When the soldiers came to seize him in the Garden of Gethsemane, Jesus told his companion to "Put your sword back in its place" (Matt. 26:52). Jesus did not resist arrest, or humiliation, or beating. And when Jesus was dying on the cross, his followers heard him say, "Father, forgive them, for they do not know what they are doing" (Luke 23:34).

Denial of the Savior

The early Christians understood the peace dimension of the gospel and obeyed the teaching and example of Jesus concerning peacemaking.

Church history tells us that the early Christians were almost uniformly pacifist. They could not visualize themselves fighting against others for whom Christ had died. No Christian writer before the reign of Constantine (312 A.D.) justified the participation of believers in warfare. Their objection to fighting was based not only on a revulsion to Roman idolatry but also on a desire to be obedient to Christ.

Unfortunately for gospel witness among Muslims, the history of Christian-Muslim encounter after the rise of Islam in the seventh century has been marked by violence. The best-known episode in that sad story is the period of the Crusades, which began nine hundred years ago. The period was finished in two hundred years, but the poisonous influence of the Crusades is with us still. Pope Urban II organized the first crusade in 1095. Armies from Europe assembled at Constantinople in 1097, marched down through Asia Minor, and captured Jerusalem with great slaughter in 1099. Four crusader states were established. One of these was recaptured by Muslims already in 1144; Jerusalem held out until 1187. There were some eight crusades in all. Their most solid military accomplishment was the capture of Acre and a strip of the Palestinian coast in 1191 and their retention for a century.

The Crusades marked a change in Christian attitudes to war. After Constantine had become emperor of the Roman Empire, Christian thinkers had developed the theory of a "just war." But even when fighting for a just cause, soldiers had been required to do penance for the deaths they caused. Before the Crusades, Pope Gregory VII proclaimed "that it was meritorious, not sinful, to fight in a just cause to promote right order in society" (Watt 1991:78).

Laurence Browne, British scholar and missionary to Muslims in Lahore, Pakistan, wrote "One cannot help regarding the Crusades as the greatest tragedy in the history of Christianity, and the greatest setback to the progress of Christ's kingdom on earth." The tragedy, wrote Browne, was that Christians denied "the Savior who bought them," and that the church approved it. "It was for Christ's honor that they fought, but they were ignorant of what sort of deeds would do honor to Christ" (1933:144).

Thou Shalt Not Kill . . . the Turk

When the Anabaptist movement began in Europe in the 1520s, the Ottoman Turks were on the move from Turkey toward Europe. They conquered Hungary in 1528 and laid siege to Vienna in 1529. Needless to say, the Austrians considered the Turks a serious threat, and public feeling was high to fight the enemy. In this situation Michael Sattler, an Austrian Anabaptist leader, made a remarkable statement about Muslims.

Sattler was the leader chosen to preside at the great Schleitheim conference on Anabaptist principles in southern Germany in 1527. But soon after he returned home from the conference, he was arrested by the Austrian authorities. The record of his trial and martyrdom was carefully preserved. One of the accusations made against Sattler was that he had said, "If the Turk were to come into the land, one should not resist him" (Yoder 1973:71). When Sattler had the chance to defend himself in court, he responded, "If the Turk comes, he should not be resisted, for it stands written, thou shalt not kill. We should not defend ourselves against the Turks or our other persecutors, but with fervent prayer should implore God that He might be our defense and our resistance" (Yoder 1973:72).

Sattler understood that the command of Jesus not to resist the evil one—and the Lord's own example of nonresistance—was the Christian's duty in relating to Muslims even when Muslims were national enemies and military aggressors. His statement to that effect was not well received amid the fear and war-fever of Austria at the time of the Ottoman invasion. How would that statement have been received among North American Christians during the more recent 1991 Persian Gulf War? Sattler's insight on fighting Muslims can be summarized in a very straightforward mission axiom: you can't tell a Muslim about the love of God in Jesus Christ and bring him into the joy of discipleship by fighting and killing him.

Choice of the Hijrah

The issues of peace and nonresistance come into sharp focus when we learn the stories of Jesus and Muhammad. Muslims themselves are well aware of the differences in the two stories. Ahmad Shawqi, a leading Egyptian man of letters in the early 1900s, wrote of Jesus:

> No threat, no tyranny, no revenge, no sword, no raids, no bloodshed Did he use in his call to the new faith. (al-Husayni 1960:300)

Such statements make an unspoken comparison. This does not mean that Muslim writers like Shawqi are comparing the Prophet of Islam unfavorably. Kenneth Cragg explains that writers like Shawqi see Jesus' life as incomplete because it lacked the political vindication and "manifest success" of the Prophet in Medina (1985b:51). Noting the contrasts between Muhammad and Jesus in the matter of violence is not considered an insult by Muslims.

The story of Muhammad's behavior in situations of conflict or suffering was set out in popular Muslim biographies such as Ibn Ishaq's *Sirat Rasul Allah* (available in Guillaume's translation *The Life of Muhammad*). According to the Muslim accounts, a major event in the life of Muhammad was his migration from Mecca to Medina called the *hijrah*. During thirteen years of preaching as a prophet in Mecca, Muhammad had seen little favorable response and had often been mistreated. In 622 A.D., he decided to migrate to Medina to take up political leadership. In Medina Muhammad became both prophet and statesman, both preacher and general, both teacher and judge. The *hijrah* meant a "flight from powerlessness in Mecca to political empowerment in Medina" (Shenk 1995:284). The English translation of Ishaq's biography devotes some 200 pages to Muhammad's fifty-two years leading up to the hijrah but gives more than 450 pages to the ten years of rule in Medina, including reports of battles, raids, intrigue, political maneuvering, assassinations, and military conquest.

The change in tone from Mecca to Medina is also reflected quite strikingly in the Qur'an as well, according to Muslim chronologies of its chapters or "surahs." Medinan surahs like "Women" (4) and "Repentance" (9), for example, contain repeated commands to fight and kill. Meccan surahs such as "Cattle" (6), by contrast, indicate a reckoning for unbelievers on the Day of Judgment, but prescribe no punishment in this life.

The Muslim biographers of Muhammad describe the Prophet's activities in Medina as positive and worthy of emulation. By human standards, Muhammad's success as a statesman and warrior in Medina must be seen as a completion of his career as a prophet in Mecca. It is only a standard "from above" which puts this behavior into question.

In his book *Muhammad and the Christian*, Kenneth Cragg works carefully at an evaluation of the Prophet of Islam. Cragg notes the tendency in Islam, above all other faiths, to place trust in political religion—to see political power and physical force as a friend that cannot be dismissed. This is a legacy of Muhammad's hijrah, Cragg concludes, the "power equation" which linked the word of God with the force of the sword. Cragg questions persistently whether force and power can accomplish the will of God. He points out that while force may ensure survival, it also generates hypocrisy. Fighting evil into submission merely makes it go underground. "The power that sanctions truth inspires deception" (1984:46). What happens to the quality of religious allegiance when people conform only because of the threat of force? Cragg asks. He uses a verse from the Qur'an, "Let the people of the Gospel decide [judge] by what God has sent down there" (5:47), to hold Muhammad up alongside "the ministry and Cross of Jesus our Lord" (159).

David Shenk summarizes this crucial gospel distinction in a helpful way:

> The Islamic understanding of the nature of the kingdom of God and the manner in which the community of peace is established and preserved is the opposite of the gospel understanding. The way of the *hijrah* and the way of the cross are fundamentally different foundations on which the respective communities, *ummah* and church, are established. The emigration of Muhammad from suffering in Mecca to political triumph in Medina and the journey of Jesus from triumph in Galilee to crucifixion and death in Jerusalem are movements in opposite directions. (1995:286)

Way of Suffering Love

> To the Christian mind, nurtured by Jesus and the Gospels, it will always be a burden and a tragedy that force has been so uncomplicatedly enshrined in the very canons of Islam via the pattern of the *Sirah*. For that sufficient reason, any appreciation of Muhammad *in situ* must resolutely retain the contrasted meaning of the love that suffers as the Christ. (Cragg 1984:51)

Cragg continues his masterful query of the compatibility of God's will with the use of physical force in *Jesus and the Muslim*. There he suggests that the temptation to take a shortcut to fulfilling the will of God came to Jesus as well. Political power was available to Jesus just as it was to Muhammad. The third temptation of the devil in the Matthew 4 account, notes Cragg, is the option for power. "Satan has Jesus visualise political empire with its compelling shortcuts to the goal and, because of these, its inevitable compromise with evil, with brutality and force." Jesus refused the temptation in the knowledge that "the Messianic task and the political arm" are not compatible (1985b:154).

But Jesus' perception went deeper, writes Cragg. His commitment to the Father in the Garden of Gethsemane, "Not my will, but yours be done" (Luke 22:42), takes into account the full measure of human evil. That evil will not be conquered simply by resisting it. Humanity will only be redeemed if its sin is vicariously borne. The death of Jesus on the cross, writes Cragg, "is the power of love that faces and undergoes the worst that we can do in sinfulness and for that very reason masters it without remainder and so accomplishes our forgiveness" (1985b:179).

Cragg asks whether a linkage of God's word with political power and physical force really reflects a realism about human evil and the remedy it requires. Restraining cannot forgive, and retaliation keeps the evil alive and even accentuates it. How then can evil be truly redeemed?

> Only "taking" wrong forgivingly, takes it away. The wrongdoer has then no cause to perpetuate his enmity, no reason to despair of himself and no occasion to entrench himself in evil. On the contrary, there is in his neighbor's "peace" that which closes the account, frees the spirit from enmity and hate, restores the broken community between the persons, and truly "overcomes evil with good." We cannot have it so, however, without knowing that a cost is born, is readily and sacrificially paid, by the soul that wills forgiveness, whose "peace" is active, compassionate and ready. (182)

This is exactly what happened in the cross of Christ, writes Cragg. And what we see in Jesus must lead ultimately to our whole concept of God. Daud Rahbar came to this conclusion after a thorough study of the theology of the Qur'an, and it led to his conversion: "When I read the New Testament and discovered how Jesus loved and forgave His killers from the Cross, I could not fail to recognize that the love He had for men is the only kind of love worthy of the Eternal God" (1960b:8).

Kenneth Cragg does not present these penetrating insights merely to make interesting observations in comparative religion. Rather, he takes pains to highlight these thoughts because they express something essential about *the nature of the gospel itself*. In his experience, the Muslim context has drawn out truths about the gospel which Christians often miss or neglect in other settings. Peace, reconciliation, and the way of the cross are essential components of the good news we share. They in turn have implications for our manner of gospel witness among Muslims.

The words of Jesus about peacemaking, and the stories about his gentleness, go out in the Muslim world with great power and invite a crucial gospel distinction. Have Christians made the peace teaching and the example of Jesus an essential part of their message to Muslims? If not, why not? Could it be because we are embarrassed about the ways in which Christians in the past have acted against the way of peace? Is it because we struggle with Christian theologies which allow for the use of physical force? Is it possible that uncritical loyalty to our countries sometimes makes us see the way of the cross as foolish and impractical?

Gospel witness among Muslims must match the gospel's peaceable nature. Witness which does not take peace into account is less than authentic. After relating the story of the dove of peace which appears at the start of this chapter, Mark Thomsen writes, "It is only as we become two-handed bearers of peace that we bear witness to God who comes not to crush the human family into conformity to God's will but who is willing to be crushed to constrain our wills and draw our hearts and minds to the . . . cross" (1996:196). That is the subject of our next chapter.

CHAPTER NINE

Peaceable Witness among Muslims

Indonesian Mennonite church leader Charles Christano tells the story of receiving a telephone call in the middle of the night. A man on the line told how his daughter had been in an accident and that she needed blood urgently. But the local hospital had no blood to give and neither had the Red Cross. The Red Cross had referred him to Charles.

"May I ask who is speaking?" said Christano.

"I'm ashamed to say," came the reply.

"Why?" asked Christano. "There's no need to be ashamed."

Hesitantly, the man gave his name, prefixed by "Haji." Christano recognized that he was speaking with an important man in the Muslim community of his Indonesian town.

"What is your daughter's blood type?" asked Christano. Then he phoned four members of his congregation whose blood matched and told them to get down to the hospital.

Because of the blood given by the Christians, and the prayer of Christano for the girl that night, the Haji's daughter survived.

One night about a month later, two vans pulled up in front of Christano's house. The Haji brought his immediately family as well as other relatives to see Christano. As a gift they brought a complete bunch of bananas, which they said was from their own tree.

"Of all the people who might have given blood at the hospital," asked the Haji, "why did it have to be you?"

"When I grew up, I was taught to hate Christians," he said, looking at Christano quizzically. "When I grew up, I was taught to hate Chinese." The Haji said that there were plenty of other Hajis in his neighborhood, but none had been willing to help.

"Why did it have to be you?"

Christano relates this story to illustrate an important principle of Christian witness to Muslims. The message of the cross—the symbol of God's unconditional love—must certainly be proclaimed to Muslims, he says. But the way in which Christians proclaim can be the deciding factor in whether the message reaches its goal. If the gospel message struck the Greeks of Paul's day as "foolishness" and the Jews as "a stumbling block," says Christano, then we shouldn't be surprised if Muslims have difficulty accepting it as well. But will the behavior of Christians, and their method of witness, make it easier or harder for Muslims to hear the words? Christano insists that the gospel must be related gently and sacrificially. If Christians approach Muslims with arrogance or lack of sensitivity, it will only make the message harder to receive.

Christano lives in a city which is a center for Muslim devotion in Indonesia. It is very difficult for a Muslim like the Haji to take a stand for Christ. But Christano works toward that goal with hope and prayer and great patience. The Haji has not taken the step of faith in Jesus Christ. For Christano, no sacrifice is too great to make that step possible.

Imitation of Christ

In the last chapter we saw that there are aspects of the gospel which are often appreciated more fully in the Muslim context. The nature of the gospel (the song) points us toward appropriate ways of communicating the gospel (singing). "The difference between the cross and the hijrah has specific and practical implications for Christians and Muslims. For the faithful church, the way of obedience to Christ is a life of suffering, redemptive love, even toward one's enemies" (Shenk 1995:286). How would these implications take practical shape in gospel witness?

When Jesus first sent out his disciples on a missionary journey he told them, "I am sending you out as lambs among wolves" (Luke 10:3). He instructed them that the first thing they were to say when they entered a house was, "Peace to this house" (v. 5). "The missionary is to be careful about his or her audience. Bless with peace those who hear. Receive peace back from those who do not hear, and leave them" (J. E. Toews 1986:13).

The New Testament attracts our attention to the way in which Jesus behaved in the face of violence, and it presents this as the example for Christians to follow in their witness. Peter writes, "To this you were called, because Christ suffered for you, leaving you an example, that you should follow in his steps" (1 Pet. 2:21). Peter also gives practical examples of actions of Jesus Christians must imitate: "When they hurled their insults at him, he did not retaliate; when he suffered, he made no threats. Instead, he entrusted himself to him who judges justly" (v. 23).

Peter, of all the eyewitnesses of Jesus' ministry, had the best chance to consider what methods of witness would match the gospel. It was Peter who forbade Jesus to go the way of the cross (Matt. 16:22). It was Peter who drew his sword in an attempt to prevent the soldiers from taking Jesus to his death. Jesus had to rebuke Peter, "You do not have in mind the things of God, but the things of men" (Matt. 16:23). Human zeal and force and technique do not accomplish 'the things of God'— because God's way is "from above." In fact, trying to solve spiritual problems with physical means often sets back our witness because it confirms prejudices and misunderstandings about the gospel. We must, like Peter, come to see the wisdom of the cross.

> The Cross, by its very quality, calls for emulation. It has to be taken up. Those who know themselves redeemed by its power are called to become themselves redeemers through its secret. . . . 'What is lacking in the sufferings of Christ' (Col. 1:24) is not their efficacy but their imitation. (Cragg 1985b:183)

In imitation of their Lord, the first Christians made a nonresistant, defenseless witness. They were ready to die making a witness to Christ, though never to kill for it. Comparing the first two centuries of the church with the first two centuries of Muslim expansion highlights peaceable gospel witness in a striking way. The spread of Islamic influence went hand in hand with military conquest. The rapid expansion of the church, by contrast, took place at a time when Christians had no access to political power and prohibited the use of force.

Beyond the Crusades

Christian leaders of later centuries drifted from the defenseless witness of the first Christians. But not all believers agreed with the church's growing use of political power and physical force. For example, during the Crusades Hubert of Romans noted that some critics were saying "that it is not in accordance with the Christian religion to shed blood in this way, even that of wicked infidels. For Christ did not act thus" (Riley-Smith 1990:80).

However, most criticism of the Crusades was directed at abuses of the movement rather than at the movement itself. At that time the only identifiable pacifist groups were the Cathars and the Waldensians—whom the Catholic Church considered heretics. But others saw at least that fighting against Muslims was not the way to spread the Christian faith. The founding of the Franciscan and Dominican orders in the thirteenth century marks the first attempt from Europe "to abandon forceful means to re-establish Christ's kingdom, and to organize missions to win converts by peaceful means" (Cooper 1985:125).

The name of Francis of Assisi is associated with this movement. He went to visit the Sultan of Egypt while the Fifth Crusade was still in progress. Defenseless, he preached the gospel to Europe's enemy (Zwemer 1949). Soon after, Franciscan monks followed his example and went to preach the gospel in northern Africa. The climax of this movement was in the work of Ramon Lull of Majorca. Lull saw the failure of the Crusades and stepped forward to boldly proclaim "the power of loving persuasion as the only means worthy of Christ" (Cooper 1985:126).

Frank S. Khair-Ullah quotes the words of Erasmus, whose writings had an influence on the thinking of the Anabaptists. "The best way and most effectual to overcome and win Turks," Erasmus wrote about 1530, "would be if they shall perceive that thing which Christ taught and expressed in His life to shine in us" (1975:821).

It is important, when thinking about Christian failings of the past, clearly to state that these actions went against the nature of the gospel itself. We may want to confess these sins on behalf of the Christians who committed them. During the late 1990s, some European-background Christians retraced the routes of the crusaders to ask forgiveness for their atrocities. We too may want to repent on behalf of the crusaders.

Nevertheless, the fact that Christians dishonored Christ in the past should not make us hesitate to honor Christ today. The gospel message was never the problem. The problem was that Christians did not obey the gospel—they did not live lives worthy of the gospel. Our hesitating to offer the gospel out of a sense of guilt will only mean that people will not hear of God's great love for them in Christ. The dishonoring of the gospel among Muslims in the past should propel us to strive to present the gospel of peace and the glory of Christ. Only in this way can the Christian mistakes of the past be undone.

Patrick Sookhdeo, an Indonesian convert to Christ, warns against contemporary methods of Christian witness among Muslims which seem to have a combative edge. He speaks against "a crusade mentality whereby we see Muslims as enemies. . . . Of the past we can only repent. In the present we must ensure that all we do is in a Christlike way" (Rabey 1996:76).

Truth without Imposition

Those who bear witness to Jesus leave their hearers full freedom to consider and respond. They rely on the power of the Holy Spirit to "convict the world of guilt in regard to sin and righteousness and judgment" (John 16:8). They may attempt to persuade the hearer of the truth, as Paul did (2 Cor. 5:11; Acts 19:8), but they don't try to coerce or manipulate or offer external inducements. "Witness comes exposed, without the power to coerce. When coercion enters in, witness is perverted. Witness seeks not its own welfare, but the welfare of the other. When methods are introduced that compromise the integrity of the other, witness is perverted" (Martinson 1996:188).

Kenneth Cragg sees a model for witness in the way in which God "commends" his love to us (Rom. 5:8). He finds in the Greek verb *sunistemi* the sense of presenting the truth peacefully in the expectation that the hearer can recognize it. "The truth has to find its acknowledgment in the other's consent" (1996:136). The Christian worker too must follow this model. "God does not 'impose his love on us'. Nor does he dictate it. Instead, he offers or invites. 'Behold I stand at the door and knock.' This is the divine pattern." This means that there is no place for imposition in Christian witness. Rather, the Christian will do everything she can to make the truth 'recognizable' for the hearer, but will then wait in faith for a favorable response. "We commend a gospel of divine love," writes Cragg (1996:139).

Paul uses the same Greek verb again in 2 Corinthians 4 when he describes his method of witness: "We have renounced secret and shameful ways; we do not use deception, nor do we distort the word of God. On the contrary, by setting forth the truth plainly we *commend* ourselves to every man's conscience in the sight of God" (v. 2). Paul considered the ministry of gospel witness a sign of God's great mercy. He did not lose heart on the basis of the response. Neither did he resort to methods out of keeping with the gospel message to produce results. He left the results to God.

Peaceable gospel witness makes a distinction between strength in the power of the Holy Spirit and the human forcefulness which cannot accomplish God's intentions. Putting our trust in skill, ingenuity, or physical methods may betray a lack of confidence in the power of God. George Brunk III describes how a proper understanding of God's role should shape our approach:

> Irenic witness to the claims of Christ is one that takes its strong, unapologetic stand on the stage of history to be seen and heard. It is

strong in commitment and conviction without resorting to psycho-logical manipulation or external coercion. Just as in instances of suffering evil we defer to the retribution of God, so in our mission, once we have shared the story of God's grace to us in Jesus, we defer to the visitation of God's spirit in the listener to persuade. An irenic witness can afford to exercise great patience while the Lord works. (1994:52)

With Gentleness and Respect

The behavior of Jesus is the standard for Christian lifestyle among Muslims. Our lives should radiate the "meekness and gentleness of Christ" which Paul refers to in 2 Corinthians 10. Paul seems to be saying that this meekness and gentleness accomplish what no physical force can do, and that is to "take captive every thought to make it obedient to Christ" (v. 5). Our lifestyle should imitate the friendliness of Jesus—his easy, natural way of relating to women, children, and men. Following Jesus means making good friendships with Muslims. Communicating our respect to these friends and showing integrity in our relationships are essential parts of good friendships.

We can find some very helpful instructions for a peaceable witness in the letters which the first missionaries wrote to the first churches. Peter wrote that Christians should always be ready to give an answer "to everyone who asks you to give the reason for the hope that you have." Then he describes the manner of this witness: "do this with gentleness and respect" (1 Pet. 3:15).

Peter's advice is highly relevant for Christian converts in an Islamic context because it was written to a community of Christians who were suffering for their confession of Jesus. Peter admonishes his readers not to respond in kind to the hostility of the opponents of the gospel. "If they would let their actions be determined by the actions of their opponents, the devil's circle of evil and hate would never be broken. The response should be determined by Christ, by his example that should be fol-lowed" (Kuitse 1985:41). Opposition was not a reason for Christians to be fearful or silent. But Peter urges them in this difficult situation to make sure their manner of witness is characterized by gentleness and respect.

> Modesty, gentleness, and courtesy (different translations of the Greek word praútes, also used in 2 Cor. 10:1) are words describing an attitude of not imposing oneself on others and taking care that the other is not hurt so that the gap does not become deeper because

of words that are misunderstood. The second word is "respect" or "reverence" (*phóbos* which also means awe or fear) for the other person—despite opposition—as a creature of God, as one for whom Christ died. An attitude of courtesy and respect is part of the way the Christian accounts for the hope that is in her or him. (Kuitse 1985:42)

Two-thirds world Christians with experience in Muslim ministry echo Peter's advice. John Mahamah, a convert from Islam to Christ in Ghana, counsels, "We need to approach people with the attitude of humility, mutual respect and the love and power of God" (1997:8). A beautiful book which arose out of the African experience, *Christian Witness among Muslims*, urges gospel messengers to avoid arguments in conversation with Muslims (1971:21-24). Samir Youssef, Arabic missionary with MBMS International, suggests that when dealing with Muslims, we "earn their trust with kindness and patience." Out of many years of experience as an evangelist in Egypt, he counsels: "Don't argue or debate with Muslims because it causes confusion; it opens the door for criticism and hatred; and it increases mutual animosity and discrimination." Youssef's advice includes a peacemaking dimension: "If you hear someone cursing you during your ministry"—for example, calling out *kafir* or heathen—"don't get upset; accept it in the spirit of love (1 Cor. 13:4-7)" (1997).

Martyr Witness

Jesus told his disciples that they would be faced with violence from religious and political authorities because of their witness, and he told them how to respond. "When you are brought before synagogues, rulers and authorities, do not worry about how you will defend yourselves or what you will say" (Luke 12:11). Jesus sent out his disciples on an essentially defenseless witness. The only power they possessed was the power of the Holy Spirit—who would give them both words and protection in the moment of danger.

Today in many Muslim countries, Christians are experiencing persecution in various ways. These include harsh living conditions under *shari'ah* or Islamic law, armed attacks by violent Muslim groups, victimization under blasphemy laws, imprisonment and assassination of Christian leaders, and harassment and killing of converts. Reports of this suffering come to us from Sudan, Iran, Egypt, and Pakistan. What response would match the gospel of peace?

When opponents of the gospel mistreat the messenger for bearing witness to Christ, or decide to kill the convert, the peace teaching of the New Testament requires a martyr witness. According to Revelation 12:11, the martyr witness of Christians is an essential part of Satan's defeat: "They overcame him by the blood of the Lamb and by the word of their testimony (*marturias*)." They use no physical weapons, but they have a spiritual weapon which is sure to overcome Satan: "They did not love their lives so much as to shrink from death."

John Mahamah reports the growth of churches in Ghana which have many members from Muslim background. The church of 200 he pastored there was three-fourths converts. He says the gospel in his context is "a message of blessing married with suffering." He adds that where people he knows are effectively planting churches in Muslim contexts, it is because they are suffering with their members (1997).

Love the Assassin

A fine illustration of what it means to minister among Muslims in imitation of Christ comes from the life of Dr. Sa'eed Kurdistani, sometimes known as the "beloved physician of Iran." Dr. Sa'eed was one of the finest medical doctors in Iran at the beginning of the twentieth century, and his story is a beautiful encouragement toward peaceable witness.

Sa'eed grew up in the northwest corner of Iran, in a region called Kurdistan. He was part of a dedicated Muslim family: His father was a Muslim religious leader, and when he passed away, Sa'eed became a *mullah* in his father's place.

Everything he heard about Christianity assured Sa'eed that Islam was superior. Then one day some Christian evangelists came to his town. One of them asked Mullah Sa'eed to teach him the Persian language. As Sa'eed spent time with this Christian, he began to see that his earlier impressions of Christianity were wrong. He learned about the good news of Jesus Christ; he also learned a lot from the truthful and humble way in which the Christians lived. One day he was especially impressed to hear them pray for God's blessing on friends and enemies alike. That surprised Sa'eed because as a mullah he was often hired to write prayers for people for the destruction of their enemies.

After much research, personal struggle, and counting the cost, Sa'eed committed himself to the Lord Jesus. Later Sa'eed received the chance to study medicine and dedicated his life to serving the people of Iran as a physician. He served anyone who needed help, whether prince or peasant. The people really liked his help, but they were continually insulting and persecuting him because he had left Islam to follow Christ.

One time he operated on the eyes of a Sultan. The surgery was successful. At just about the same time a Muslim leader sent a letter asking Dr. Sa'eed to come to him so that he could "explain Sa'eed's difficulties and dispel his doubt."

Dr. Sa'eed sent back a bold—but typical—response that "I have no doubts, but rather I'm certain. Perhaps it is you who need the assurance which Christianity provides."

This reply made the Muslim leader angry. He hired a notorious assassin named Mahmud Khan to kill Dr. Sa'eed. When Dr. Sa'eed left the Sultan to go to another town, the road through the mountains was so dangerous that the Sultan sent with him an armed escort of fifty men.

The Muslim leader meanwhile told the assassin to intercept Sa'eed on that road and put him to death. When the Sultan got wind of the assassination plot, he sent his fastest messenger to the caravan to tell them to go by another route. Sa'eed was saved.

Many years later, Dr. Sa'eed set up his practice in the city of Teheran. One day a man in an army uniform came to his home suffering from an abscess on his neck. Dr. Sa'eed was conducting a Bible reading at the time, so he greeted the visitor in a friendly way and asked him if he minded waiting until the Bible reading was finished.

On completing the reading, Dr. Sa'eed left the room to sterilize a scalpel. After a moment of silence, the army captain spoke to the others: "You gentlemen don't know me. Many years ago I tried to kill this man, but this is the way he has treated me and my relatives all these years."

Dr. Sa'eed helped the man. When the man left, the others asked the doctor to explain. Dr. Sa'eed told them, "The man you have just seen is Mahmud Khan, the notorious bandit of Kurdistan. Once when I was traveling in a caravan in the mountains, a Muslim leader sent this man along with a band of his henchmen to kill me, but God's mercy preserved us by a change of route."

In the years in between, Mahmud Khan and twenty-five members of his family had been confined in a house in Teheran for a year and a half. During this time, Dr. Sa'eed had served as their family physician free of charge (Rasooli & Allen 1983:176).

Let our Methods Match

Dr. Sa'eed of Iran dedicated his life to serving people who were continually insulting him and trying to kill him for his loyalty to the

Lamb. He knew only the power of the Lamb—that power that comes from the Lamb laying down his life, forgiving his killers from the cross, and being slain to take away the sin of the world.

Some strategists may say that Dr. Sa'eed's way of witness can't amount to much. They might call for more aggressive and focused methods. But the beloved doctor's story is worth reflecting on. Iran is a difficult country. During the last two decades of the twentieth century, the mightiest countries of the world have been unable to force Iran to change even its foreign policy! Is there any military power on earth which can accomplish the will of Jesus for the Muslims of Iran? No, the weapons of this world cannot make disciples for Jesus. But the power of unconditional love in action and readiness to die for the gospel of peace will win and already have begun to win the hearts of Iran's people for Jesus Christ.

Can we learn to trust God that matching our methods to the gospel's peaceable content will be the best way to proceed in witness among Muslims? The nature of the gospel itself points us in the direction of vulnerability and sacrifice. Can we "follow the Lamb wherever he goes" (Rev. 14:4)? For Christians who would serve Jesus among Muslims today, the challenge is great.

> The deeply humbling fact remains that the Muslim world (specifically the Muslim, Arabic-speaking world) has never in its whole history had a chance to see the Christian church as she is according to her true nature and calling but has always been presented with lamentable caricatures. The church's opportunity is now here. The great question is this: will the opportunity be taken? If so, then a new dimension of thinking and of spiritual and intellectual preparation emerges and as it does so calls for new inventive answers and a new kind of commitment. (Kraemer 1960:251)

CHAPTER TEN

Spiritual Dynamics of Ministry

A bou Traore is an evangelist from the Samogho people who has been discipled by missionaries from the Africa Inter-Mennonite Mission. Before becoming a follower of Jesus, Abou had been a sorcerer.

Abou knew the secrets involved in sorcery and worked together with Muslim leaders in the larger towns of Burkina Faso, explains Loren Entz. Whenever a Muslim leader was approached by someone willing to pay for help in getting revenge, or perhaps desiring a certain woman, or wanting to make money, Abou was called in. Abou did whatever was necessary to manipulate the evil spirits to do their work.

Not long after his conversion to Christ, Abou began to be challenged by people who wanted to test the power of his Jesus. Entz tells how Abou was invited by elders from his own tribe. The elders first tried to kill Abou by poisoning his food. Abou said a prayer of thanks before he ate and suffered no ill effects. Then the elders led him to their sacred grounds late at night and placed him beside a gaping hole. Fire escaped from the hole. One of the elders whistled in a special way and poisonous bees emerged from the pit. But they could not harm Abou.

Their final test was one from which no one else had escaped. They summoned a huge snake which came toward Abou. It tried to push him into the pit as it had pushed in many before. But the snake could only brush his leg. The snake itself fell into the pit. There was no doubt that God's power working through Abou was greater than that of the fetishes through the village elders. The rest of the night Abou preached the good news of Jesus to the elders of his tribe (Entz 1986:46-48).

There is a spiritual conflict at work whenever we proclaim the gospel to people. It takes place behind the human relationships that we can see. This is also true in Muslim settings. We must take this dimension of ministry seriously and try to understand it better. The New Testament gives us a lot of practical information about the reality and activity of what it calls "the powers of this dark world." We can also learn a great deal from Christian workers in the Muslim world who have experience in this area.

God has given us many resources for ministry in the midst of spiritual conflict. The nature of some of these resources may in fact surprise us. We tend to think of power and overcoming in human terms. But God has chosen "the weak things of the world to shame the strong" (1 Cor. 1:27). We find that the weapons which God gives would have to be judged very ineffective by human standards. Yet, because God gives them, these spiritual resources have "divine power" to accomplish the goal of ministry as nothing else can.

Considering the spiritual dynamics of ministry in Muslim contexts causes us to acknowledge our deep need of God's Holy Spirit. Without the Holy Spirit, we would have no power to bear witness to Jesus Christ in the first place. God gives his Holy Spirit to us for this very purpose. "The work of the Holy Spirit is the most vital part of Muslim evangelism," says Irani evangelist Reza Safa. "To not recognize His office and His part is to labour in vain" (1996:69a).

Called to Take a Stand

Scripture teaches that Christian workers have a serious enemy in Satan. The devil "prowls around like a roaring lion looking for someone to devour" (1 Pet. 5:8). Jesus was familiar with the activity of spirits which he called "evil" and "unclean." He also spoke of the devil, calling him a "murderer from the beginning." Satan tempted Jesus and opposed his mission. Christians who seek to make disciples for Jesus become involved in a spiritual conflict. Paul wrote that the missionary struggles "against the rulers, against the authorities, against the powers of this dark world and against the spiritual forces of evil in the heavenly realms" (Eph. 6:12).

In this spiritual battle, Christians are called to take a stand. The immediate goal is defensive—to withstand the attack of the devil: "Resist the devil, and he will flee from you" (James 4:7). In order to help Christians hold their ground, God gives them a full suit of spiritual armor (Eph. 6:10-18).

The conflict in gospel witness is not a fight between the good guys and the bad guys—as in a Hollywood movie. Rather, it is a spiritual conflict in which the human soul is at stake. The battle is for the hearts and minds of humans. And, unlike some popular works of fiction, the focus in Scripture is not on the battle between God and Satan. That battle has already been won. Rather, God desires to win back to himself those humans who joined Satan in his rebellion. "The battle rages in the human heart, which God and Satan seek to win" (Hiebert 1994:211). God pursues the rebels by love, truth, and the assurance of forgiveness and reconciliation.

Christian workers must be realistic about the reality of dark spiritual forces. They should be alert and aware of the activity of Satan to prevent people coming to Christ. But they must also avoid an undue fascination with, and fear of, Satan and his hosts. That might cause them to take their eyes off of Jesus, their strength (Hiebert 1994:214).

We have no need to fear Satan, because the One who is in us is greater than the one who is in the world (1 John 4:4). Jesus came to earth to destroy the works of the devil (1 John 3:8). He gives disciplemakers the promise of his living, risen presence (Matt. 28:20). God has not given us a spirit of timidity, but rather a spirit of power, of love and of self-discipline (2 Tim. 1:7) Our outlook on spiritual conflict should match the confidence of Paul when he wrote, "The Lord will rescue me from every evil attack and will bring me safely to his heavenly kingdom" (2 Tim. 4:18).

Weapons of the Spirit

Sometimes when we use the imagery of warfare to describe the spiritual dynamic of Christian life and ministry, we may begin to think that what is needed is a harshness or combativeness on our part, or perhaps a mastery of technology or technique. We need to be careful not to let the very influential ideas about power in our culture pervert the New Testament meaning of spiritual warfare. And for Christians in ministry, one of the most damaging ideas is that the way to solve the problems of evil in this world is to exert more force than the evil person.

In 2 Corinthians 10:3-4, Paul refers to weapons which people use in this world. Weapons of death and destruction can be very impressive and can accomplish a great deal in physical terms—even more so now than in Paul's time. But Paul takes for granted that these physical weapons are powerless to help us accomplish God's mission. The weapons we need for ministry among Muslims are not those of the world. Physical weapons don't work because we are not fighting people but rather spiritual forces of evil.

The struggle of gospel witness is *not* against flesh and blood, Paul specifies. We do *not* wage war as the world does. The weapons given for ministry are *not* the weapons of this world. Rather, God gives spiritual weapons which have divine power "to demolish strongholds" (2 Cor. 10:4)

When we examine the various items of the "full armor of God" listed in the New Testament, they appear quite ineffective by the world's standards: truth, righteousness, the gospel of peace, faith, salvation, the word of God, and prayer in the Spirit. Yet these are the very weapons which allow Christians to be strong in the Lord's mighty power. Spiritual weapons are effective where physical weapons are not because they solve problems which go deeper than any others.

A good example of how spiritual weapons work is the case of the "word of God." Paul calls it "the sword of the Spirit" (Eph. 6:17). Hebrews tells us that the word of God is sharper than any double-edged sword because "it penetrates even to dividing soul and spirit, joints and marrow; it judges the thoughts and attitudes of the heart" (4:12).

A sword can very effectively cut through bone and marrow—but no more. The word of God, on the other hand, doesn't harm the body but gets right through to the thoughts and intentions of the heart. This is where the real battle is.

The Gospel is Dynamite!

A good gauge of the true nature of spiritual conflict is that one of the weapons of the Spirit is the *gospel of peace*. Paul writes that the good news about Jesus is the power of God for the salvation of everyone who believes (Rom. 1:16). The Greek word for power is *dunamis*, from which we get our English word dynamite. The gospel is spiritual dynamite which is able to work in the hearts and minds of people beyond our presence and witness. Thank God for that because we ourselves sense how weak and limited our own personalities and proclamation can be!

The gospel is the story of how Jesus gave his life to make peace between God and humanity as well as among humanity's warring tribes. This gentle story of reconciliation has amazing power to save people (1 Cor. 15:2). Paul was careful in his missionary work not only to preach the gospel but also to let its full power emerge through him. He wrote that he did not preach with words of human wisdom, because he wanted the peoples' faith to rest on the power of God. "For I resolved to know nothing while I was with you except Jesus Christ and him crucified" (1 Cor. 2:2).

Those who bear witness to Christ in the Muslim world must trust God that their clear proclamation of the gospel is God's power to save Muslims. God sends out his word with a purpose, and it will not return to him empty. If we see no short-term response, we must be patient and be willing to repeat the good news "in season and out of season" (2 Tim. 4:2), as Paul instructed Timothy. There is much we do not see or understand. The gospel is veiled to many. To some it is a stumbling block, to others it just sounds foolish. Paul writes that "the god of this age has blinded the minds of unbelievers, so that they cannot see the light of the gospel of the glory of Christ" (2 Cor. 4:4). When Paul preached, his gospel proclamation did not always draw a positive response. But he did not let that cause him to lose heart in gospel witness, nor did he let lack of response tempt him into putting his trust in human methods.

Power of the Lamb

The supreme event in spiritual warfare is the cross, where the Son of God laid down his life for the sins of the world. Paul writes that through the cross God "disarmed the rulers and authorities making a public example of them" (Col. 2:15). On the cross Christ gave up his life, even though he had but to utter one command and ten thousand angels would have come to his rescue. If our understanding of spiritual warfare does not have the cross at its center, it is wrong.

The New Testament uses the image of the lamb to draw attention to the defenseless spiritual power of the cross. When, in the vision of Revelation 5, there is a search for someone who is worthy to open the scroll, the elder announces that "the Lion of the tribe of Judah" has triumphed. However, in the vision we see a Lamb, "looking as if it had been slain" (v. 6). The Lamb is worthy above all others because he was slain, and with his blood "bought men for God from every tribe and language and people and nation" (v. 9). From that point till the end of the Bible, Jesus is known only by his name "the Lamb." As Wesley Prieb notes about the Bible's astonishing closing vision, "Lamb power will win!" (1986:127).

The Power of the Lamb is none other than that which comes from the Lamb laying down his life and being slain for the sins of the world. Satan's defeat comes not by self-assertion on the part of Jesus, but by self-sacrifice. It was through his death that Jesus destroyed the devil (Heb. 2:14). This important point comes out clearly in Revelation 12:11. There, the way in which Jesus' disciples defeat Satan is "by the blood of the Lamb and by the word of their testimony; they did not love their lives so much as to shrink from death."

It turns out that the weapons which are most effective against Satan are the self-sacrifice of Jesus and the imitation of that self-sacrifice by his disciples. Many early Christians laid down their lives making a "martyr witness" to Jesus. Persecuted Christians throughout history have known the power of "not loving their own lives so much as to shrink from death." The Anabaptist movement in sixteenth-century Europe never grew so quickly as during the first 50 or so years of intense persecution. "It looked as if the persecutions made their numbers increase," wrote Nanne van der Zijpp (1984:121). Many similar stories could be cited from our own century. The Meserete Kristos Church in Ethiopia was forced underground by the Marxist government during the 1980s but emerged 10 years later with 10 times the membership (Shenk 1994:149).

Between 1996 and 1998, more than 100 churches were burned by Muslims in Indonesia. But the persecution resulted in church growth. "Our Muslim leader in Indonesia has been telling his people to stop burning our churches and to start reading history," said Andreas Christanday of Indonesia, chair of the Asia Mennonite Conference. "He tells the people that the more they torture Christians . . . the more they will grow" (Oswald 1998:21).

Power Encounter in Conversion

When Muslims become disciples of Jesus, they go through a major spiritual struggle. Conversion involves a deliverance from one kingdom and a transference into another. Jesus told Saul that his future mission work would involve turning Gentiles "from the power of Satan to God" (Acts 26:18). Paul later wrote that God the Father "has rescued us from the dominion of darkness and brought us into the kingdom of the Son he loves" (Col. 1:13). We can also picture conversion as being freed from the 'force field' of sin into the 'magnetic' influence of Jesus Christ.

The process of transference into the kingdom of God does not come easily, because every individual wants to maintain human autonomy. "The central issue in God's confrontation of any man," says Arthur Glasser, "is his authority and Christ's Lordship. This means 'power encounter'—for the divine power that confronts and woos is inevitably resisted by the human spirit." For a Muslim, this encounter includes transcending many years of hearing that Jesus is merely a human prophet to revere, one in a long chain of prophets stretching from Adam to Muhammad. To acknowledge Jesus as the one true Lord of the universe involves a spiritual struggle. "When the whole thrust of the gospel is that Jesus Christ is not to be admired only, but 'received' with a transfer of allegiance—submitting to his rule—the trauma of conversion is inevitable" (Glasser 1979:133).

Strongholds of the Soul

Very close under the surface of Orthodox Islam are a variety of common practices which fall into the category of what Paul Hiebert calls the "excluded middle" between the theological and the natural (1994:196f.). It is common for Muslims to go to *pirs, sayyids, sheikhs*, and other religious leaders for supernatural help. Many make pilgrimages to the tombs of leaders from the past who were reputed to have power. They go for help with felt needs at the everyday level: for physical healing, finding a suitable spouse for a child, for barren women to conceive, to curse enemies or for protection from curses, and perhaps even to try to rearrange predestined fate. They look for help in manipulating powers not at the theological level but at a felt-needs level.

Bill Musk details many of these supernatural practices in *The Unseen Face of Islam*. He finds that many Muslims live in a world which is far from the orthodox Islam of most Western textbooks. They confess faith in Allah, but fear spirits. Rick Love suggests that three-fourths of the Muslim world, about 800 million people, are "doctrinally Muslim but functionally animist" (1998:17).

Whenever people go to occult practitioners for help, they open themselves up to the influence of dark spiritual forces and give permission—consciously or unconsciously—to these powers to possess and enslave them. Paul uses the expression "stronghold" to picture the captivity in which many people live (2 Cor. 10:4). They are not free to respond fully to God because they live under the oppression of evil spiritual powers. A church in Africa which is evangelizing Muslims has found that most converts from Islam have previously been possessed by evil spirits through contact with Muslim sheikhs. New believers need to be freed from these controlling spirits (A. H. and M. B. 1998:34).

What about Islam itself? Would it be accurate to describe this religion as a spiritual "stronghold?" Religions in general exist as systems in rebellion against God (Hiebert 1989:56). Even in the Gospels, religion is "the central citadel of [humanity's] desire for self-fulfillment and therefore of [human] resistance to the God whose being is self-emptying" (Newbigin 1982:107). But Paul further qualifies strongholds as "arguments and every pretension that sets itself up against the knowledge of God" (2 Cor. 10:5). Islam is certainly a major fortress in the world, holding nearly one billion people in its strong walls. Does Islam help people to get to know the true God as he has revealed himself in Jesus Christ? Or is it a power which works against the knowledge of God? Does Islam help to direct the thoughts of people to make them "obedient to Christ?" Or does it hold back the thoughts of people from this obedience?

Some Christian workers among Muslims ask why the Qur'an and its Muslim exegetes would deny the death of Jesus on the cross. What is the spiritual dimension of this denial? According to the gospel, the death of Jesus is the great source of blessings for the world, including salvation, forgiveness of sins, and eternal life. Why would Islam want to so decisively deny Jesus' Sonship and his divinity, not allowing him to be more than a human prophet? Why forbid to people a relationship with the One who is Life? Why discourage people from calling on Jesus as Lord—thereby denying them the rich blessings of God (Rom. 10:12)?

As we ask such questions, we need to show special care. African Christians of Muslim background seem to be especially sensitive to the way we characterize Islam spiritually. John Mahamah notes how quickly Western writers such as Peter Wagner and George Otis Jr. judge Islam to be demonic. Mahamah says, "I wonder whether too much attention is not ascribed to Satan whenever Islam particularly is brought into focus" (1997:7). Ethiopian Mennonite leader Bedru Hussein suggests that this approach can go against our witness: "Because of such an attitude, Muslims immediately raise barriers and do not listen to us" (1993:11).

When speaking of the spiritual conflict behind the visible dimensions of mission, we need to be careful not to begin to speak about people with disrespect. Disrespect represents nothing more than a simple prejudice. We must resist this temptation. Muslims are people whom God loves and for whom Christ died. We share the same humanness and reliance on God's grace.

Supernatural Ways

If folk Islam, with its occult practices, is a vital part of the lives of most ordinary Muslims, then Christian workers must develop a biblical response to the questions they face. First of all, Christians can proclaim freedom from the power of spirits and witchcraft through the greater power of the living Christ. This is good news for most Muslims.

Second, our invitations to Muslims to follow Christ should also include demonstrations of God's power. Some workers may shy away from this area of ministry if it is unfamiliar, but God can enable us by his

Holy Spirit. "Missionaries must not be reluctant to join the spiritual battle on the deepest levels," writes Ken Peters. "Because Muslim mystics believe in signs and wonders, we must confront them with the power of the true and living God" (1989:368).

Sometimes the churches in Africa and Asia show the way for European-background workers with their Enlightenment baggage. David Shenk found in Indonesia that

> power encounter is the normal manner in which the church is growing. Several significant Muslim leaders have been converted and this has dramatically influenced the profile of the Christian-Muslim encounter. Divine healings and exorcism are part of the normal Christian witness in Indonesia. (Quoted in K. Peters 1989:368)

Christian workers must cultivate a readiness to pray for healing and to let Jesus show his power in supernatural ways. The healing power of Jesus was an important factor in the conversion of Sister Gulshan Esther, a Pakistani woman. She tells the remarkable story of her encounter with Jesus and her healing from paralysis in *The Torn Veil*.

Paul Hiebert points out that while demonstrations of God's power draw attention to Jesus, they bring no easy victory. Some will see them and believe, but others will respond with greater hostility. In the life of Jesus, the religious leaders often treated his miracles as reasons to oppose him. In the book of Acts, most signs and wonders led to imprisonment and death. "When we are involved in power encounters, we must be ready to pay the price, for the cross is the paradigm of how God works in human history" (1989:57). Hiebert also urges workers not to go ahead of God's leading in attempting public demonstrations of power, "for such demonstrations fail and discredit God if he is not in them" (1989:60).

The key in all of our ministry is prayer. Prayer is the spiritual weapon highlighted by Paul; it is the weapon of radical dependence on God alone. "Prayer is the supernatural way of opening closed doors and human hearts for effective evangelism. As Christians we have to pray earnestly without ceasing so that the control of the power of darkness over people may break" (Hussein 1993:12). When Tokumboh Adeyemo became a Christian, he discovered that through the power of the Holy Spirit he could live for Christ, tell others about him, and be victorious. "I started seeing results of prayer. Yet I had nothing—no talisman, no magic—just the name of Jesus Christ!" When his people saw this, they started calling him nicknames like "prophet" or "son of Jesus." But as a result of seeing Christ's power, they started moving from hostility to skepticism and later to neutrality and some to faith in Christ (Adeyemo 1989:229).

Christian workers want Muslims to come into a relationship with Jesus Christ. Therefore they plead with God the Father to draw people to His Son in any way He might choose: through them, or without them, or despite them; through a verbal witness to Christ or through an act of kindness; through dreams and visions or healings and other miracles. There is no need to neglect any of the ways which God may use. And we must not hesitate to consider unfamiliar ways if this is the direction the Holy Spirit is leading.

Goal Is Obedience to Christ

The goal of spiritual warfare is to bring every thought of every person into obedience to Christ, according to 2 Cor. 10:5. This is an objective which simply cannot be accomplished "from below"—by the weapons of this world. We must acknowledge our deep dependence on the "power from on high" which God alone can give. We need to be careful never to think and act as if gospel witness is a matter of our own skill or ingenuity.

Of course, we must do our best to remove the human and cultural barriers which keep Muslims from coming to Christ. We must design the best tools for ministry, contextualize our message, and indigenize the church. But to think that we have thereby achieved our goal would be a misreading of Islam. Islam is more than a matter of culture and social structures. As George W. Peters wrote, "Islam is foremost a spiritual force, a theological formulation and a 'theocratic' structure." Islam is equal to all the technical skills and other human pressures which Christians may bring to bear.

> It will yield to nothing short of the Spirit of God, incarnated in a message and men, a message which expresses God as Father and as manifested and magnified in and through Christ Jesus, crucified, risen, ascended and glorified, and men who know their God and labor in the irresistible power and patience of the Holy Spirit. (G. W. Peters 1979:401)

In spiritual warfare we are fighting for the hearts and minds of people. Jesus wants us to make disciples for him. He himself came to seek and to save the lost, to give his life as a ransom for many, and to buy back people for God from every background. Now he gives us many spiritual resources for ministry through his living presence. The weapons at our disposal are not the weapons of this world. But then, earthly weapons are useless in this mission. The one who commanded us to make disciples of all nations invites us to tap into his own power, the "divine power" which alone can accomplish the goal—and that is the power of the Lamb.

CHAPTER ELEVEN

Planning for Faithful Ministry

For fifteen years the International Missions workers worked among their Muslim friends, pouring out their hearts and souls and trying every conceivable ministry which might point those around them to Jesus. But they did not see a single Muslim come to faith in Christ during that period. They did not give up, however, because they lived under God's call to be faithful.

Then something happened which has been rare in the history of gospel witness among Muslims. Between their fifteenth and twenty-third years of witness, hundreds of Muslims in their town made decisions for Christ. A church was planted, comprised of Muslim converts with indigenous leadership. By 1992 some 4,500 people in their country of service were taking Bible correspondence courses because of their ministry.

"What if they had quit earlier?" asks missions director Pat Cate. He suggests that Christian workers like these are needed in countries "where quick, easy responses are not forthcoming." The Muslim world needs workers "who believe that God's standard is faithfulness, not immediate results" (Cate 1992:231).

What is needed in ministry to Muslims is commitment to the basics of gospel witness and readiness to persevere when results seem discouraging. We have stories of fine workers in the past to point us the right direction. These workers encourage us with eloquent testimonies of the joy and privilege of working among Muslims. Recent decades have brought a rich harvest of insight from Christians from several continents and from diverse theological backgrounds who have experienced Islam in a variety of settings. They offer hope of fruitful ministry and make suggestions for how to become more effective in witness. Many of the proposals emerge from insights gained from the social sciences. They counsel paying close attention to culture and adapting both witness and worship to suit the Muslim context.

This growing body of insightful testimonies and hopeful suggestions can help Christians plan responsibly for ministry. Without planning, not much happens in mission, notes David Shenk. "God honors planning" (1994:159). Out of the many good planning suggestions, this chapter will present just a selection.

One expression frequently used to describe mission planning is "strategy." This expression is useful as long as it is in harmony with the gospel's song of peace. The term strategy comes from the Greek *strategos* or "general." Strategy is a word associated with a calculated military campaign. In a military campaign, notes Wilbert Shenk, the "other" is an enemy who is to be forcibly subdued by any means available. But as we have seen, the only warfare in gospel witness is spiritual. Any physical harshness would detract from our witness. "Neither the goal nor the means employed in a military operation are appropriate to Christian mission" (W. Shenk 1993:218-19).

There is cause for concern here: can the imagery of spiritual warfare influence us—even unconsciously—toward thinking we will accomplish our task through physical means? Careful handling of war imagery is critical in the Muslim world, where the history of the Crusades looms in the background, and where the Western political and economic imperialism of recent centuries is a fresh memory (D. Shenk 1983:145).

One other caveat is that planning for effective ministry among Muslims is not the property of European-background thinkers. Yes, a great deal of writing about mission strategy has been coming from North America. But in the meantime, churches in Africa and Asia have been quietly finding ways to evangelize and disciple the Muslims around them (cf. A. H. and M. B. 1998; D. Shenk 1983:154-155; Nazir-Ali 1987:85-89; Mahamah 1997; Hussein 1993; Christano 1982). We need to highlight, wherever possible, the insights which these newer churches are ready to share. And North Americans need to be aware when their own cultural values enter unquestioned into their mission strategies.

Lessons of Experience

The apostolate to Islam has been blessed with some of the strongest workers in the history of Christian mission. These missionaries have prepared thoroughly for their ministry, worked hard to develop relationships with Muslims, and lovingly and tactfully presented the gospel to individuals and small groups. Surveying this history, G. W. Peters has made an appropriate tribute. "I marvel," he says, "at the devotion, the insights, the thoroughness, the depth—theological, missiological and methodological—the versatility, adaptability and the innovation which these saints of God manifested in their ministry" (1979:390).

Throughout the past 100 years of Christian witness in Muslim settings, missionaries have learned many lessons about what is helpful and what is harmful. Many workers have emerged from decades of dedicated service in the Middle East, Africa, or Asia to write about their experiences. We must pay attention to what these veterans are telling us so that we don't think we have to reinvent the wheel. Christian workers from many different church traditions and national backgrounds have worked with all their heart, mind, and strength to bear witness to Christ and to make disciples among Muslims.

Lyle L. Vander Werff's detailed study of Anglican and Reformed missions to Muslims in India and the Near East leads him to two towering figures of gospel witness among Muslims, W. H. T. Gairdner and Samuel Zwemer (1977). He finds in their many decades of ministry in the Middle East a depth of wisdom about evangelistic approach; a sensitive, sympathetic understanding of Islam; and a lively appreciation for the role of the church.

Direct Personal Contact

The foundation of faithful ministry among Muslims is a commitment to the basics of gospel work. First of all, there is deep love for Muslims as people whom God created in his own image. God wants all Muslims to come to a knowledge of the truth of the gospel. Jesus laid down his life and rose again so that Muslims could be free of the power of sin and the fear of death, and become his disciples. The worker needs a sense of the call of God to communicate this gospel message despite difficulties. The quality of life of the witness is also crucial. "Does that life radiate *agape* or does it bespeak ulterior motives?" (W. Shenk 1981:20).

Faithful ministry begins with strong and friendly relationships with people and expresses itself in an incarnational style modeled on the example of Jesus. It means living among Muslims as their neighbors and fostering relationships of love. Experience has shown that evangelism among Muslims calls for a long-term wholistic commitment to them in their particular cultural situations. Patience and perseverance are at the heart of faithful ministry among Muslims.

Hendrik Kraemer laid a great deal of emphasis on the character of the missionary. The best method for gospel witness, he wrote, is "direct personal contact and study of the Bible in a spirit of human sympathy and openness" (1938:356). He urged Christians in such relationships to treat their Muslim friends not as non-Christians but rather as fellow human beings with the same fundamental needs, aspirations, and frustrations. Missionaries need to respect Muslims and regard their religious experiences and insights as every bit as worthwhile as their own, Kraemer wrote.

Pakistani church leader F. S. Khair-Ullah counsels a kind of fellowship with Muslims which takes a long-term view:

> The best of modern missionaries to Islam pursue a mode of approach which was seldom neglected by their predecessors but which was never quite trusted to bear full fruit—the method of intimate personal friendship, of loving service, of sympathetic testimony, and of united prayer. (1975:824)

When Dan and Helen Nickel began a gospel witness in a Muslim section of Hyderabad, India, in 1984 under MBMS International, they followed a simple threefold approach. In their immediate neighborhood they shared their faith in the midst of friendships. They teamed up with a Muslim convert, John Mahboob, to offer an Urdu-language Bible correspondence course through Muslim newspapers. This allowed anonymity to individual Muslim seekers who wanted to learn about the Bible. Dan also taught Muslim evangelism to future pastors and evangelists at the Indian Mennonite Brethren Bible Institute. His hope was that these church leaders would catch a vision for witness among the Muslims in the villages where they would be assigned. "Most of the 3,000 villages affected by the India MB Church have Muslim residents—some as high as 50 percent," he found (1985:15).

Samuel Zwemer also considered faith conversation in the context of personal relationships to be the highest and noblest method to winning a hearing for the gospel among Muslims. Zwemer had in mind conversation of a very high quality, explains G. W. Peters: "personal friendship evangelism highly motivated, carefully cultivated, prudently and prayerfully prepared and persistently followed through" (1979:393).

Pay Attention to Culture

In recent years, Christian workers have made many valuable suggestions for how to communicate the gospel in such a way that it can be clearly understood by Muslims. They have made use of insights from the social sciences about the local cultural situation or context. Out of this research, they offer practical ways to contextualize the gospel and the faith expressions of new Christians. They suggest that by paying closer attention to Muslim cultures, missionaries can avoid some of the misunderstandings of the past. "Contextualization seeks to express the Christian faith in a way which is both true to Scripture and relevant to the cultural context of the recipients" (Eenigenburg 1997:310).

Motivation to search for new and effective ways to bring Muslims to Christ comes partly from the observation that conversions of Muslims to Christ have been very few compared to what happens in some other cultural and religious contexts. Some question whether earlier approaches have been relatively ineffective because missionaries have not given adequate attention to historical and cultural barriers.

Many of the suggestions prompted by social science insights are well worth keeping in mind in formulating a responsible strategy. Here are a few of the very basic insights.

1. *Relate the gospel in the terms of the audience.* Look for ways to connect with what Muslims already know and believe. Become familiar with the theological vocabulary which Muslims use to describe their faith and try to learn the precise sense of each word. David Shenk prepared a Bible study series for Muslims called the *People of God* in response to the request of a Muslim friend in Somalia. He wanted to be able to offer the teachings of the Bible in a format which respected Muslim knowledge of biblical revelations and characters. While preparing the curriculum, he asked, "What is the core of the Muslim worldview and the nature of Islamic culture?" (1994:198).

2. *Identify the cultural baggage of the Christian worker.* Missionaries sometimes come with beliefs and practices which have more to do with their home cultures than with the gospel. Traditions such as sitting in pews must not be imposed on new Christians in Muslim cultures. And if the cultural practices of missionaries make it difficult for Muslims to open their hearts to Christ, they should be sacrificed. This is an area in which there is room to remove unnecessary hindrances. Phil Parshall's comparison of popular perceptions of Muslim leaders and Christian missionaries indicates some of the possibilities for creative adaptation (1983:116-118).

3. *Be alert to felt needs.* Beyond the ideal Islam of the Five Pillars is a large area of popular Islam which reveals the personal everyday needs of human beings (Inniger 1979; Musk 1979). Christian workers must recognize these needs and tune their gospel witness to the heart and

emotions in addition to the intellect. The gospel offers the answer to a wide range of human needs. We should look to apply the gospel at the point where it is most relevant. This will lead us to a more sensitive appreciation of important areas of culture (Musk 1995; cf. Thomas 1994) and will open our eyes to the extent to which ordinary Muslims have sought for occult powers in an effort to find satisfaction of felt needs.

4. *Explore ways to celebrate together.* Sharing in cultural celebrations is a helpful way to strengthen friendships. We should participate in local cultural and even in religious observances to make it easier for Muslims to hear our message. For example, some Christian workers say that observing the Muslim fast during Ramadan has drawn them closer to the Muslims they live among (Speers 1991; cf. A. Fast 1995:4). The commendable desire to get closer to Muslims, of course, needs to be balanced by a realism about how such actions are perceived by Muslims themselves. We also need to consult the local church to learn the local wisdom and to avoid becoming a cause of offense.

5. *Freedom in worship forms.* Christian workers can explore ways to enable new believers to practice their faith meaningfully and relevantly. There are many spiritually neutral cultural forms in Islamic societies which can be used. African and Asian workers such as Rafique Uddin are giving guidance in the use of forms with which Muslims are familiar (1989; cf. D. Shenk 1983:154-155; Abdol Massih 1979:90-92). How can converts come to feel happy and fulfilled in their worship of God through Jesus Christ?

6. *Minimize the isolation of the convert from her home.* Who is better able to reach family and friends with the gospel than the convert herself? Are there ways in which we can work so that Muslim converts can possibly stay in their families and original neighborhoods to carry on a witness there? In other religious and cultural settings, converts remain in their home communities and their gospel witness works out naturally to their family and friends. The strong Muslim concept of community solidarity makes this more difficult. In any case we must question the impulse to automatically "extract" new Christians from their community.

Build with Good Materials

Beyond the above ideas for making the gospel understandable to Muslims and removing unnecessary obstacles from their paths, some have made proposals which take contextualization into uncertain areas. For example, some missionaries have begun to call themselves Muslims in an effort to identify with their hosts. One team in the Middle East has a policy of not allowing missionaries to identify themselves as Christians (Eenigenburg 1997:311). Another trend is to encourage new believers in Jesus to remain part of the Muslim *ummah* rather than joining the Christian church. That may include the nurturing of a "Jesus mosque" deliberately distinct from existing Christian congregations in the area. It also may include maintenance of five-times-daily ritual prayer, sometimes in the local mosque, using a modified version of the Islamic *Salat* prayer formula.

The more extreme proposals of what Gary Corwin has called "super-contextualization" have brought a corresponding call for greater discernment. Some workers have begun to apply the concept of "critical contextualization" in ministry among Muslims. Some of the questions being asked come from a desire to safeguard the integrity of the gospel messenger and to avoid deception in our method. Some ask whether the more extreme theories take into account the reality that the gospel is an offense to some. Another question which should be asked is whether a New Testament concept of church would keep Muslim converts separate from the body of Christ! The questions come from Christians who want Muslims to meet Christ, and who want to avoid using unworthy materials in building on the gospel foundation. "Each one should be careful how he builds" (1 Cor. 3:10).

Can a cultural orientation to technique and expediency cause Western Christian workers to slide over difficult theological questions? InterServe director James Tebbe finds this to be the case in the cross-cultural work of evangelicals. He suggests that avoiding the tough theological questions for pragmatic reasons leads to retreat and defensiveness in ministry. He urges a clear theological position. "As we are confident of a firm ground on which to stand, we will be able to draw close to Muslims without fear. In our theological understanding we can find clear confidence" (1996:174). What theological touchstones can help us discern strategy proposals?

Integrity of the worker

The Christian worker must be above reproach in honesty and personal transparency. Her yes must be yes, and her no, no (Matt. 5:37). "I know it is popular in some circles to affirm, 'Yes, I am a Muslim,' under the rubric that the word merely means one who is submitted," says Episcopal missions leader Kevin Higgins. "But this is not putting the messenger in context. It lacks a deeper integrity, though it is true enough semantically" (Guthrie 1998:221).

Truthfulness in method

We have noted in earlier chapters Paul's resolute repudiation of deception (2 Cor. 4:2; Eph. 4:25). When we enter Muslim cultures, we must study what constitutes deception in the eyes of the local people, especially with regard to religion, and then avoid all appearances of deception. We may find that local people evaluate Christian workers by a more stringent standard then they would judge themselves (Racey 1996:308).

Spiritual discernment

Scripture commands us to test the spirits to see whether they are from God (1 John 4:1). In the spectrum of cultural forms which are part of Muslim societies, where do neutral forms end and spiritually charged forms begin? Parts of Islam are clearly incompatible with the gospel (Eenigenberg 1997:314). Muslims themselves say that all of life is part of their religion. Is it realistic to argue that Islam is merely a neutral cultural entity rather than a religious entity with spiritual commitments?

Beauty of the body

In an effort to make it possible for new believers to remain part of the Muslim community, some workers have proposed innovative concepts of conversion and models of church (Teeter 1990; Brislen 1996; cf. Kraft 1979; Parshall 1980:157-180). But do these proposals match the New Testament vision of the body of Christ? The homogeneous unit principle, for example, has been strongly challenged from the New Testament (Padilla 1983). Are the beauty and unity of the body important considerations in the new proposals? "Contextualization must never be a camouflage for the presence of the church, and it must be deeply sensitive to the need for identity with the universal church" (D. Shenk 1983:153).

Cost of discipleship

Workers have also looked for ways to remove unnecessary suffering from the lives of new believers. Some of the difficulties which converts face have been for cultural or political reasons rather than for the sake of the gospel. But much of the ostracism and persecution come because the convert has declared loyalty to Jesus Christ. Jesus himself said that those who follow him will experience difficulty. Is there a danger of tampering with discipleship? Samuel Zwemer was emphatic on this point:

Unless we ask the Moslem enquirer to make a clear-cut decision, to break with his past to accept a new way of life in Christ, we are really doing him an injustice. The easy way is not the way of the Gospel. A friendlier attitude toward Christ and Christianity is not enough. The way of the Cross means crucifixion, not inoculation. (Quoted in G. W. Peters 1979:401)

Genuine points of contact

The search for bridges, keys, or redemptive analogies must be accompanied by a determination to build only with strong materials. Hendrik Kraemer questioned whether points of contact between the gospel and Islam are as easy to find as some have suggested. Religions are self-contained systems which give their own meanings to theological terms. Using the same terms does not signify a point of contact. For example, the Isawa people of northern Nigeria are attached to 'Isa, the Qur'anic version of Jesus. But they are not in fact particularly receptive to the New Testament affirmations of the divinity and redemptive death of Jesus (Gilliland 1997:9).

Appeal to the Mind

The strategy help which the social sciences provide could leave us with the impression that this is the limit of the worker's creativity. But there are many other encouragements. Workers from Asian and African cultures often see opportunities because of their native knowledge of local ways. These opportunities include appeals to the mind and imagination. When Daud Rahbar became a Christian in 1960, he urged the church to reach out in a special way to well-educated, committed Muslims—because these have influence in their respective societies. He believed that exploring theology itself would be a profitable area of Muslim-Christian encounter (1960a; 1961).

Fouad Accad counseled the use of the Qur'an and its commentaries to draw the attention of Muslims to passages which indicate that Jesus is more than a prophet and miracle-worker (1976). He argued that since Muslims give authority to the Qur'an and not to the Bible, the Qur'an is the appropriate place to begin to make a case for Christ. Accad modeled and spelled out an effective use of the Qur'an in seven "Muslim-Christian principles" (1997).

There is also room for missionaries to work in the more sophisticated imaginative areas of culture. How many missionaries get to know the culture well enough to reach the hearts and minds of intellectuals?

Michael Nazir-Ali notes a tendency among some missionaries to confuse identification with the indigenous culture with identifying with the very poor. He urges a greater identification with values such as indigenous classical music and local literature. "Many missionaries, however, never go beyond the acquisition of a rudimentary knowledge of a local language. They have no real encounter with the art, music and literature of the country in which they live and where they have been called to serve" (1983:155).

When I was learning Urdu in Karachi, my teacher, Mr. Agha Ata, suggested something which amazed me at the time. He said that to reach his circle of highly cultured Urdu-speaking friends with the gospel, all that a missionary would need to do is to learn Urdu well enough to compose one beautiful long poem—a *ghazal*—about Jesus Christ. He said that if the missionary were able to successfully recite this poem at a poetry gathering attended by the cultural élite, he could then pack up and return to his country of origin. The impact on this influential group would be sufficient to justify the missionary's time, effort, and expense. At the time I was focused on long-term incarnational ministry. Agha Sahib said I could accomplish my mission with a single good poem.

Later Agha Sahib and I worked together to compose a drama for a Christmas program to which we would invite our Muslim friends. We wrote a parable of Jesus' incarnation out of a famous Muslim story of a king who left his palace at night to mix with the common people in the bazaar. We took the story further to show that a Good Emperor would feel compassion for the people he ruled, and would even sacrifice his own life out of his deep love for them. Agha Sahib rendered the script into a faultless courtly Urdu. The Muslims who saw this drama were left with a powerful story which could work in their imagination to open a door for a theological concept which Islam resists. At the end of the performance, the lead actor came to the front of the stage and boldly read John 1:1-14.

Use other Helpful Means

Christian workers from around the world are offering suggestions which give hope for fruitful witness and help the church to plan responsibly for faithful ministry. In addition to the suggestions referred to above are many other ideas worth taking into consideration. Leaders of the Frontiers mission have worked hard to develop principles of church planting in Muslim cities, and they recommend that Christians minister there in the form of teams (Brown 1997; Livingstone 1993). David Shenk and Ervin Stutzman also affirm the team approach and emphasize the characteristics of the apostolic church (1988).

Other workers have written about entry into restricted-access Muslim countries through legitimate professional or business "tentmaking" work. In some regions, radio is widely listened to and can be a powerful medium to communicate the good news. Muslims can listen in the privacy of their homes and respond in writing to the broadcaster. In other areas where people can afford satellite receiving dishes, Christian TV programming could be effective. The Jesus video distributed by Campus Crusade for Christ has possibly been the medium used by God to lead more Muslims to faith in Christ in recent years than any other media tool. It has been translated into almost every major Muslim language (Cate 1992:234).

In all of our mission planning, our standard for faithful ministry is not the insights of the social sciences, the latest missiological trend, or even the lessons of experience, but rather the Word of God. We have a duty to ask whether strategy suggestions, whether they are said to work or not, have a sound biblical basis. We should resist the temptation to put our trust in technique or technology when we feel challenged by the difficulties of Muslim ministry. Rather, we should strive to be obedient. From a kingdom perspective, the only valid criterion of authentic mission is faithfulness, not success (D. Shenk 1983:154).

We also need to make sure that our methods match our message. "In Christ, means and ends converge," writes David Shenk. "Any technique or plan which is not immersed in love and genuine concern for the totality of the other person must be condemned" (1983:154). Mission must be pursued in the constraints of the gospel. "In mission the manner is the message. The cross embraces the world, but only at the price of its own hurt. The wounds of Christ wait to win, they do not grab to take. Can it be otherwise with the faith, the church, the mission, that bear his name and 'desire all nations?'" (Cragg 1989:21).

In that sure orbit of the gospel of peace there is plenty of room for hope and creativity in gospel witness among Muslims. Tokumboh Adeyemo, out of his African experience, challenges Christian workers to move ahead confidently in a peaceable approach: "With love in our hearts, tears in our eyes, purity in our lives, justice in our hands and power on our heads, we must boldly take the gospel of peace and offer it to every Muslim. May the Lord help us!" (1989:230).

References

EMQ - Evangelical Missions Quarterly
ERT - Evangelical Review of Theology
IBMR - International Bulletin of Missionary Research
IRM - International Review of Mission
MBH - Mennonite Brethren Herald
MF - Mission Focus
MQR - Mennonite Quarterly Review
MW - The Muslim World
UM - Urban Mission

A. H. and M. B. 1998. "Refugees Evangelizing Muslims." *UM* 15:31-36.

Abdol Massih, Bashir. 1979. "The Incarnational Witness to the Muslim Heart." In *The Gospel and Islam*, ed. Don M. McCurry, 85-96. Monrovia, Calif.: MARC.

Accad, Fouad Elias. 1975. "God at Work in Circumstances: Personal Meetings (Acts 8:26-40)." In *Let the Earth Hear His Voice*, ed. J. D. Douglas, 51-53. Minneapolis: World Wide Publications.

———. 1976. "The Qur'an: A Bridge to Christian Faith." *Missiology* 4:331-342.

———. 1997. *Building Bridges: Christianity and Islam*. Colorado Springs: Navpress.

Adeyemo, Tokumboh. 1989. "Social and Theological Changes in Conversion." In *Muslims and Christians on the Emmaus Road*, ed. J. Dudley Woodberry, 219-230. Monrovia, Calif.: MARC.

Adrian, Victor. 1994. "Jesus and the Religions of the World." *Direction* 23:29-43.

Augsburger, Myron S. 1962. "Conversion in Anabaptist Thought." *MQR* 36:243-57.

Baker, Ken. 1990. "Power Encounter and Church Planting." *EMQ* 26:306-312.

Balic, Smail. 1979. "The Image of Jesus in Contemporary Islamic Theology." In *We Believe in One God: The Experience of God in Christianity and Islam*, ed. Annemarie Schimmel & Abdoldjavad Falaturi, 1-8. London: Burns & Oates.

Bardai, Aly. 1997. "The Truth About Jesus." *Encounter* (*MBH* special edition, Spring/Summer): 21-22.

Bosch, David J. 1983. "The Structure of Mission: an Exposition of Matthew 28:16-20." In *Exploring Church Growth*, ed. Wilbert R. Shenk, 218-248. Grand Rapids: Eerdmans.

———. 1991. *Transforming Mission: Paradigm Shifts in Theology of Mission*. Maryknoll, N.Y.: Orbis, 1991.

———. 1994. "The Vulnerability of Mission." In *New Directions in Mission and Evangelization, 2, Theological Foundations*, ed. James A. Scherer and Stephen B. Bevans, 73-86. Maryknoll, N.Y.: Orbis.

Bradshaw, Bruce. 1988. "Integrity and Respect Are Keys To Muslim Witness." *EMQ* 24:358-362.

Brislen, Mike. 1996. "A Model for a Muslim-Culture Church." *Missiology* 24:355-367.

Brown, Dan. 1997. "Is Planting Churches in the Muslim World 'Mission Impossible?'" *EMQ* 33:156-161.

Browne, Laurence E. 1933. *The Eclipse of Christianity in Asia*. Cambridge: University Press.

Brunk, George III. 1994. "The Exclusiveness of Jesus Christ." In *New Directions in Mission and Evangelization, 2, Theological Foundations*, ed. James A. Scherer and Stephen B. Bevans, 39-54. Maryknoll, N.Y.: Orbis.

Burkholder, Byron. 1981. "No Safer Place." *MBH* (October 9): 21.

———, ed. 1984. *They Saw His Glory: Stories of Conversion and Service*. Winnipeg, Man.: Kindred Press.

Calverley, Edwin E. 1952. "Samuel Marinus Zwemer." *MW* 42:157-159.

Cate, Pat. 1992. "What Will It Take to Win Muslims?" *EMQ* (July): 230-234.

Chacour, Elias, with David Hazard. 1984. *Blood Brothers: A Palestinian's Struggle for Reconciliation in the Middle East*. Eastbourne, Sussex: Kingsway.

Chapman, Colin. 1989. "Biblical Foundations of Praying for Muslims." In *Muslims and Christians on the Emmaus Road*, ed. J. Dudley Woodberry, 305-322. Monrovia, Calif.: MARC.

————. 1995. *Cross & Crescent: Responding to the Challenge of Islam*. Leicester, England: InterVarsity Press.

Christano, Charles. 1982. "PIPKA: An Indonesian Response to Mission." *IBMR* 6:169-172.

Christensen, Jens. 1979. *The Practical Approach to Muslims*. Marseille: The North Africa Mission.

Christian Witness Among Muslims. 1971. Achimota, Ghana: Africa Christian Press.

Cook, Michael. 1983. *Muhammad*. Oxford: Oxford University Press.

Cooper, Anne, comp. 1985. *Ishmael My Brother*. Monrovia, Calif.: MARC.

Cragg, Kenneth. 1980a. "Being Christian and Being Muslim: A Personal Debate." *Religion* 10:196-208.

————. 1980b. "Conversion and Convertibility—With Special Reference to Muslims." In *Down to Earth: Studies and Culture and Christianity*, ed. John R. W. Stott and Robert Coote, 193-208. Grand Rapids: Eerdmans.

————. 1981. "Temple Gairdner's Legacy." *IBMR* 5:164-167.

————. 1984. *Muhammad and the Christian: A Question of Response*. Maryknoll, N.Y.: Orbis.

————. 1985a. *The Call of the Minaret*. 2d ed. Maryknoll, N.Y.: Orbis.

————. 1985b. *Jesus and the Muslim*. London: George Allen & Unwin.

————. 1989. "Contemporary Trends in Islam." In *Muslims and Christians on the Emmaus Road*, ed. J. Dudley Woodberry, 21-43. Monrovia, Calif.: MARC.

————. 1996. "A Christian Among Muslims." *ERT* 20:136-140.

Dehqani-Tafti, H. B. 1982. *Design of My World: Pilgrimage to Christianity*. New York: Seabury.

Dyck, Cornelius J. 1984. "The Anabaptist Understanding of the Good News." In *Anabaptism and Mission*, ed. Wilbert R. Shenk, 24-39. Scottdale, Pa.: Herald Press.

———. 1995. *Spiritual Life in Anabaptism: Classic Devotional Resources.* Waterloo, Ont.: Herald Press.

Eenigenburg, Dan. 1997. "The Pros and Cons of Islamicized Contextualization." *EMQ* 33:310-315.

Entz, Loren. 1986. "Challenges to Abou's Jesus." *EMQ* 22:46-50.

Ewert, David. 1995. *A Testament of Joy: Studies in Philippians.* Winnipeg, Man.: Kindred.

Fast, Alfrieda. 1995. "Four Muslim Women." *MCC Women's Concerns Report* 120: 2-4.

Fast, Heinold. 1983. "The Anabaptist Understanding of Jesus' Great Commission." *MF* 11:4-7.

Faw, Chalmer E. 1993. *Acts. Believers Church Bible Commentary.* Waterloo, Ont.: Herald Press.

Friesen, Herb. 1996. *A Reluctant Surgeon.* Published privately in Pakistan.

Friesen, LeRoy. 1992. *Mennonite Witness in the Middle East: A Missiological Introduction.* Elkhart, Ind.: Mennonite Board of Missions.

Friesen, Randy. 1995. "Why Have You Forgotten Us?" *The Christian Leader* 58 (August): 10.

Gerber Koontz, Gayle. 1996. "Evangelical Peace Theology and Religious Pluralism: Particularity in Perspective." *The Conrad Grebel Review* 14:57-85.

Ghulam, Masih Naaman. 1990. *My Grace is Sufficient for You.* Rikon, Switzerland.

Gilliland, Dean S. 1997. "Principles of the Christian Approach to an African-Based Islamic Society." *Missiology* 25:5-13.

Glasser, Arthur F. 1976. "Is Friendly Dialogue Enough?" *Missiology* 4:261-266.

———. 1979. "Power Encounter in Conversion from Islam." In *The Gospel and Islam,* ed. Don M. McCurry, 129-142. Monrovia, Calif.: MARC.

Goldsmith, Martin. 1976. "Community and Controversy: Key Causes of Muslim Resistance." *Missiology* 4:317-323.

———. 1982. *Islam & Christian Witness.* Downers Grove, Ill.: InterVarsity Press.

Good, Merle. 1994. "Bedru Hussein: Gentle and Intense." *Festival Quarterly* (Winter): 12-13.

Grady, J. Lee. 1996. "A Shiite Muslim's Story." *Charisma* (September): 71.

Green, Stanley W. 1990. "Anabaptism and Ecclesiology in a Context of Plurality." *MF* 18:23-25.

Guillaume, A., trans. 1955. *The Life of Muhammad*. Trans. of Ishaq's *Sirat Rasul Allah*. Karachi: Oxford University Press.

Gulshan, Esther, and Thelma Sangster. 1984. *The Torn Veil*. Basingstoke, Hants, U.K.: Marshall Pickering.

Guthrie, Stan. 1998. "Just saying No." *EMQ* 34:218-223.

Habib, Gabriel. 1990. "Renewal, Unity, and Witness in the Middle East: An Open Letter to Evangelicals." *EMQ* 26:256-260.

Hamm, Peter M. 1967. "A Reappraisal of Christianity's Confrontation with Other Religions." In *The Church in Mission*, ed. A. J. Klassen, 222-250. Hillsboro: Mennonite Brethren Board of Christian Literature.

Hange, Roy. 1994. "Rebuilding Old Walls: A Survey of Religious Violence in the Middle East." *MF: Annual Review* 2:9-24.

———. 1996. "Healing 'Holy Hatred': Biblical and Practical Reflections." *MF: Annual Review* 4:63-73.

Hardaway, Gary. 1996. "Pioneer Medical Workers Finish 28 Years in Middle East." *MBH* (September 13): 12-13.

Heffening, W. 1993. "*Murtadd* (apostate)." In *The Encyclopaedia of Islam*, Vol. VII, ed. C. E. Bosworth et al, 635-6. Leiden: E. J. Brill.

Heidebrecht, Werner A. 1980. "Conversion in the Church Context." In *Conversion: Doorway to Discipleship*, ed. Henry J. Schmidt, 73-85. Hillsboro, Kan.: MB Board of Christian Literature.

Hesselgrave, David J. 1990. "Christian Communication and Religious Pluralism: Capitalizing on Differences." *Missiology* 18:131-138.

Hiebert, Clarence. 1967. "World Missions and Ministries of Compassion." In *The Church in Mission*, ed. A. J. Klassen, 345-360. Fresno, Calif.: MB Board of Christian Literature.

Hiebert, Paul G. 1978. "The Kingdom Reconciling Humanity." *MBH* (October 13): 6-8.

———. 1980. "Conversion in Cross-Cultural Perspective." In *Conversion: Doorway to Discipleship*, ed. Henry J. Schmidt, 88-98. Hillsboro, Kan.: MB Board of Christian Literature.

———. 1987. "Critical Contextualization." *IBMR* 11:104-112.

———. 1989. "Power Encounters and Folk Islam." In *Muslims and Christians on the Emmaus Road*, ed. J. Dudley Woodberry, 45-61. Monrovia, Calif.: MARC.

———. 1994. *Anthropological Reflections on Missiological Issues*. Grand Rapids: Baker.

Hoover, Jon. 1994. "Theological Foundations for Dialogue with Islam." *MCC Peace Office Newsletter* 24/5:1-2.

al-Husayni, Ishaq Musa. 1960. "Christ in the Qur'an and in Modern Arabic Literature." *MW* 50:297-302.

Hussein, Bedru. 1993. "Current Islamic Expansion in Africa." Paper presented to General Council Meeting of Mennonite World Conference in July. Bulawayo, Zimbabwe.

Inniger, Merlin W. 1979. "Getting to Know Their 'Heart Hunger' Is a Key to Reaching Muslims." *EMQ* 15:35-39.

Ismail, Zafar. 1983. "The Muslim Convert and the Church." *IRM* 72:385-392.

Jacobs, Donald R. 1980. "Conversion and Culture: An Anthropological Perspective with Reference to East Africa." In *Down to Earth: Studies and Culture and Christianity*, ed. John R. W. Stott and Robert Coote, 131-145. Grand Rapids: Eerdmans.

Jones, L. Bevan. 1953. "A Love that Persists." *MW* 43:3-6.

———. 1996. "How a Sufi Found his Lord." *ERT* 20:115-125.

Kasdorf, Hans. 1975. "Anabaptists and the Great Commission in the Reformation." *Direction* (April): 305-18.

———. 1980. *Christian Conversion in Context*. Kitchener, Ont.: Herald Press.

———. 1984. "The Anabaptist Approach to Mission." In *Anabaptism and Mission*, ed. Wilbert R. Shenk, 51-69. Scottdale, Pa.: Herald Press.

Kateregga, Badru D., and David W. Shenk. 1997. *A Muslim and a Christian in Dialogue*. Scottdale, Pa.: Herald Press.

Kerr, David A. 1996. "Mission and Proselytism: A Middle East Perspective" *IBMR* 20:12-22.

Khair-Ullah, Frank S. 1975. "Evangelism among Muslims." In *Let the Earth Hear His Voice*, ed. J. D. Douglas, 816-824. Minneapolis: World Wide Publications.

———. 1976. "Linguistic Hang-Ups in Communicating with Muslims." *Missiology* 4:301-316.

———. 1979. "The role of local churches in God's redemptive plan for the Muslim world." In *The Gospel and Islam*, ed. Don. M. McCurry, 566-576. Monrovia, Calif.: MARC.

Kivengere, Festo. 1975. "The Cross and World Evangelization." In *Let the Earth Hear His Voice*, ed. J. D. Douglas, 400-404. Minneapolis: World Wide Publications.

Kraemer, Hendrik. 1938. *The Christian Message in a Non-Christian World*. Grand Rapids: Kregel.

———. 1960. "Islamic Culture and Missionary Adequacy." *MW* 50:244-251.

———. 1962. *Why Christianity of all Religions?* Philadelphia: Westminster.

Kraft, Charles H. 1979. "Dynamic Equivalence Churches in Muslim Society." In *The Gospel and Islam*, ed. Don M. McCurry, 114-124. Monrovia, Calif.: MARC.

———. 1991. "What Kind of Encounters Do We Need in Our Christian Witness?" *EMQ* 27:258-265.

Kuitse, Roelf S. 1981. "When Christians and Muslims Meet." *MF* 9:1-4.

———. 1985. "Witness: 'Accounting for the Hope in Us' (1 Peter)." *MF* 13:41-42.

Lawton, Kim A. 1997. "Faith Without Borders: How the Developing World Is Changing the Face of Christianity." *Christianity Today* 41 (May 19): 39-49.

Littell, Franklin H. 1984. "The Anabaptist Theology of Mission." In *Anabaptism and Mission*, ed. Wilbert R. Shenk, 13-23. Scottdale, Pa.: Herald Press.

Livingstone, Greg. 1993. *Planting Churches in Muslim Cities: A Team Approach*. Grand Rapids: Baker.

Love, Rick. 1998. "Muhammad, Materialism, Magic, or the Messiah?" *UM* 15 (March): 15-21.

Madany, Bassam. 1979. "What Do You Say to 120 Muslims?" *Eternity* (March): 30-32.

Mahamah, John. 1997. "Global Clues for Multicultural Ministry: An African Perspective." Paper presented to Evangelical Missiological Society Conference, Caronport, Saskatchewan, May 24.

Marsh, Charles R. 1975. *Share Your Faith with a Muslim*. Chicago: Moody.

———. 1980. *The Challenge of Islam*. London: Scripture Union.

Martinson, Paul Varo. 1996. "Dialogue and Evangelism in Relation to Islam." *Word & World* 16:184-193.

Masood, Steven. 1986. *Into the Light: A Young Muslim's Search for Truth*. Bromley, Kent, U.K.: STL Books.

"The Mass Media and Church Planting in Restricted Access Countries." 1993. *EMQ* 29:278-283.

Maududi, Abul Ala. 1994. *The Punishment of the Apostate According to Islamic Law*. Trans. Syed Silas Husain and Ernest Hahn from the Urdu 1963 edition. Toronto.

McCurry, Don M. 1976. "Cross-Cultural Models for Muslim Evangelism." *Missiology* 4:267-283.

———. 1980. "Why are Muslims so Militant?" *Christianity Today* (March 21): 24-27.

Meihuizen, H. W. 1984. "The Missionary Zeal of the Early Anabaptists." In *Anabaptism and Mission*, ed. Wilbert R. Shenk, 88-96. Scottdale, Pa.: Herald Press.

Mensah, Muhammadou. 1989. "Holistic Ministry Among the Poor." In *Muslims and Christians on the Emmaus Road*, ed. J. Dudley Woodberry, 85-103. Monrovia, Calif.: MARC.

Musk, Bill A. 1979. "Popular Islam: The Hunger of the Heart." In *The Gospel and Islam*, ed. Don M. McCurry, 208-215. Monrovia, Calif.: MARC.

———. 1989. *The Unseen Face of Islam: Sharing the Gospel with Ordinary Muslims*. Eastbourne, Sussex: MARC.

———. 1995. *Touching the Soul of Islam: Sharing the Gospel in Muslim Cultures*. Crowborough, England: MARC.

Naim, C. M. 1996. "Getting Real about Christian-Muslim Dialogue." *Word & World* 26:179-183.

Nasr, Seyyed Hossein. 1998. "Islamic-Christian Dialogue—Problems and Obstacles to be Pondered and Overcome." *MW* 88:218-237.

Nazir Ali, Michael. 1983. *Islam: A Christian Perspective*. Exeter: Paternoster.

———. 1987. *Frontiers in Muslim-Christian Encounter*. Oxford: Regnum.

Newbigin, Lesslie. 1982. *The Light Has Come: An Exposition of the Fourth Gospel*. Grand Rapids: Eerdmans.

———. 1988. "A Sermon Preached at the Thanksgiving Service for the Fiftieth Anniversary of the Tambaram Conference of the International Missionary Council." *IRM* 78:325-331.

———. 1989. *The Gospel in a Pluralist Society*. Grand Rapids: Eerdmans.

Nickel, Dan. 1980. "A Witness to Muslims in Indonesia." *MBH* 19/3 (February 1): 6-7.

———. 1985. "Muslim Ministry Comes Full Circle." *The Christian Leader* (December 24): 14-15.

Nickel, Gordon. 1991. "What if You Find They're Good?" *The Christian Leader* (July 30): 11-12.

———. 1991. "With No Other Authority." *Witness* (MBMS International) (September/October): 9-10.

———. 1994. "Confessing Jesus as Lord in a World of Many Loyalties." *MBH* 33 (November 11): 4-5.

———. 1994. "Making a Gospel Witness to Muslims." *MBH* 33 (November 11): 6-8.

———. 1994. "Singing above the Azan." *Christian Week* (December 13): 13.

———. 1996a. "How Does Peace Theology Affect Our Encounters with Islam?" *The Conrad Grebel Review* 14:115-118.

———. 1996b. "Jesus Reveals His Glory." *MBH* (July 19): 6-7.

———. 1997. "A Cross and a Dove." *Witness* (MBMS International) (May-June): 1-2, 4.

Nida, Eugene A. 1960. *Message and Mission*. N.Y.: Harper & Brothers.

Ostermann, Eduard. 1980. *Er zerbricht die Mauer: Mohammedaner finden Jesus—eine Herausforderung für uns alle*. Neuhausen-Stuttgard: Hänssler.

Oswald, Laurie L. 1998. "Persecution Fuels Church Growth." *Canadian Mennonite* 2 (March 16): 21-22.

Padilla, C. René. 1983. "The Unity of the Church and the Homogeneous Unit Principle." In *Exploring Church Growth,* ed. Wilbert R. Shenk, 285-303. Grand Rapids: Eerdmans.

Parshall, Phil. 1980. *New Paths in Muslim Evangelism.* Grand Rapids: Baker.

———. 1983. *Bridges to Islam: A Christian Perspective on Folk Islam.* Grand Rapids: Baker.

———. 1985. *Beyond the Mosque: Christians within Muslim Community.* Grand Rapids: Baker.

Penner, Erwin. 1990. *The Power of God in a Broken World.* Winnipeg: Kindred.

Peters, George W. 1979. "An Overview of Missions to Muslims." In *The Gospel and Islam,* ed. Don M. McCurry, 390-404. Monrovia, Calif.: MARC.

Peters, Ken. 1989. "Touching the Mystical Heart of Islam." *EMQ* 25:364-369.

Prieb, Wesley J. 1986. "The Power of the Lamb." In *The Power of the Lamb,* ed. John E. Toews and Gordon Nickel, 117-127. Hillsboro, Kan.: Kindred.

Rabey, Steve. 1996. "Mission-Minded Design Strategy for Muslim World." *Christianity Today* (March 4): 76.

Racey, David. 1996. "Contextualization: How Far Is too Far?" *EMQ* 32:304-309.

Rahbar, Daud. 1958. "The Call of the Minaret—a Review." *MW* 48:40-51.

———. 1960a. "The Christian Message and the Muslim Intellectual Today." Address to Commission on Ecumenical Mission and Relations. New York: United Presbyterian Church U.S.A., February 9.

———. 1960b. "A Letter to Christian and Muslim Friends." Hartford, Conn.: published privately.

———. 1961. "Urgent Issues in Christian-Muslim Encounter." Paper for Division of Studies of the World Council of Churches.

Rahman, Hafizur. 1990. "Prayers and Public Morality." *MIDASIA* (November 25): 11.

Rahman, S. A. 1972. *Punishment of Apostasy in Islam*. Lahore: Institute of Islamic Culture.

Ramseyer, Robert. 1990. "Sixteenth-Century Insights and Contemporary Reality: Reflections on Thirty-Five Years in Mission." *MF* 18:21-23.

Rasooli, Jay M., and Cady H. Allen. 1983. *Dr. Sa'eed of Iran*. Pasadena: William Carey.

Riley-Smith, Jonathan, ed. 1990. *The Atlas of the Crusades*. New York: Facts on File.

Roemmele, Michael. 1993. "Cloak-and-Dagger Tentmakers Need Not Apply." *EMQ* 29:164-169.

Rudvin, Arne. 1976. "The Concept and Practice of Christian Mission." *IRM* 65:374-384.

———. 1979. "The Gospel and Islam: What Sort of Dialogue is Possible?" *Al-Mushir* 21:82-123.

Safa, Reza F. 1996a. "Christ in the House of Allah." *Charisma* (September): 68-70.

———. 1996b. *Inside Islam: Exposing and Reaching the World of Islam*. Orlando, Fla.: Creation House.

Sanneh, Lamin. 1982. "Christian Experience of Islamic Da'wah." In *Christian Mission and Islamic Da'wah*, 52-65. Leicester, U.K.: The Islamic Foundation.

———. 1984. "Muhammad, Prophet of Islam, and Jesus Christ, Image of God: A Personal Testimony." *IBMR* 8:169-174.

———. 1995. "Christian Missions and the Western Guilt Complex." *ERT* 19:393-400.

———. 1996. *Piety & Power: Muslims and Christians in West Africa*. Maryknoll, N.Y.: Orbis.

Schäufele, Wolfgang. 1984. "The Missionary Vision and Activity of the Anabaptist Laity." In *Anabaptism and Mission*, ed. Wilbert R. Shenk, 70-87. Scottdale, Pa.: Herald Press.

Schlorff, Samuel P. 1981. *Discipleship in Islamic Society*. Toronto: North Africa Mission.

———. 1993. "Muslim Ideology and Christian Apologetics." *Missiology* 21:173-185.

Sheikh, Bilquis, with Richard Schneider. 1978. *I Dared to Call Him Father*. Waco, Tex.: Chosen Books.

Shenk, Calvin E. 1986. "Conversion in Acts: Implications for Witness to Religions." *MF* 14:1-5.

———. 1992. "Who Do You Say that I Am?" *Gospel Herald* (September 8): 1-3, 7.

Shenk, David W. 1981. "The (Sufi) Mystical Orders in Popular Islam." *MF* 9 (March): 5-9.

———. 1983. "The Muslim Umma and the Growth of the Church." In *Exploring Church Growth*, ed. Wilbert R. Shenk, 144-156. Grand Rapids: Eerdmans.

———. 1994. *God's Call to Mission*. Scottdale, Pa.: Herald Press.

———. 1995. *Global Gods*. Scottdale, Pa.: Herald Press.

Shenk, David W., and Erwin R. Stutzman. 1988. *Creating Communities of the Kingdom*. Kitchener: Herald Press.

Shenk, Wilbert R. 1981. "Editorial." *MF* 9:20.

———. 1983. "Opposition to the Apostolic Witness in Acts." *MF* 11:52-54.

———. 1993. "Mission Strategies." In *Toward the 21st Century in Christian Mission*, ed. James W. Phillips and Robert T. Coote, 218-234. Grand Rapids: Eerdmans.

Smith, Jay. 1998. "Courage in Our Convictions: Debating Muslims." *EMQ* 34:28-35.

———. 1998. "Reaching Muslims in London: Is It Time to Confront?" *UM* 15 (March): 37-46.

Snyder, Howard A. 1975. "The Church as God's Agent in Evangelism." In *Let the Earth Hear His Voice*, ed. J. D. Douglas, 327-351. Minneapolis: World Wide Publications.

Speers, John. 1991. "Ramadan: Should Missionaries Keep the Muslim Fast?" *EMQ* 27:356-359.

"Spotlight on London (Jay and Judy Smith)" and "Challenging the Truth." 1995. *Therefore Go Ye* (Summer): 3-4, 10-11.

Stacey, Vivienne. 1976. "Toward a Current Strategy: Discerning God's Hand in Islam Today." *Missiology* 4:363-372.

———. 1986. *Christ Supreme over Satan: Spiritual Warfare, Folk Religion and the Occult*. Lahore: Masihi Isha'at Khana.

———. 1988. *Practical Lessons for Evangelism among Muslims*. London: Interserve.

———. 1989. "The Practice of Exorcism and Healing." In *Muslims and Christians on the Emmaus Road*, ed. J. Dudley Woodberry, 291-303. Monrovia, Calif.: MARC.

Stauffer, Ethelbert. 1945. "Anabaptist Theology of Martyrdom." *MQR* 19:179.

Sultan, Muhammad Paul. 1978. *Why I Became a Christian*. Rev. ed. Bombay: Gospel Literature Service.

Syrjänen, Seppo. 1984. *In Search of Meaning and Identity: Conversion to Christianity in Pakistani Muslim Culture*. Vammala: The Finnish Society for Missiology and Ecumenics.

Tebbe, James. 1996. "Schizophrenic Evangelicals." *EMQ* 32:173-174.

Teeter, David. 1990. "Dynamic Equivalent Conversion for Tentative Muslim Believers." *Missiology* 18:305-313.

"Tentmaking: the Road to People's Hearts." 1992. *EMQ* 28:26-29.

Terry, John Mark. 1996. "Approaches to the Evangelization of Muslims." *EMQ* 32:168-173.

Thiessen, Bill. 1995. "A Place of Birth." *MBH* 34 (December 8): 32.

Thomas, Bruce. 1994. "The Gospel for Shame Cultures." *EMQ* 30:284-290.

Thomsen, Mark W. 1993. *The Word and the Way of the Cross: Christian Witness among Muslim and Buddhist Peoples*. Chicago: Division for Global Mission, Evangelical Lutheran Church in America.

———. 1996. "The Christian Mission in the Muslim World." *Word & World* 16:194-202.

Toews, J. A. 1967. "The Anabaptist Involvement in Missions." In *The Church in Mission*, ed. A. J. Klassen, 85-100. Fresno, Calif.: Mennonite Brethren Board of Christian Literature.

Toews, John E. 1996. "Toward a Biblical Perspective on People of Other Faiths." *The Conrad Grebel Review* 14:1-23.

Toews, John E., and Gordon Nickel, eds. 1986. *The Power of the Lamb*. Winnipeg: Kindred.

Uddin, Rafique. 1989. "Contextualized Worship and Witness." In *Muslims and Christians on the Emmaus Road*, ed. J. Dudley Woodberry, 267-272. Monrovia, Calif.: MARC.

Usman, K. M. 1996. "How a Maulvi Found Peace." *ERT* 20:182-185.

van Bracht, Thieleman J., comp. 1951. *The Bloody Theatre or Martyrs Mirror of the Defenseless Christians*. Scottdale, Pa.: Mennonite Publishing House.

van der Zijpp, N. 1984. "From Anabaptist Missionary Congregation to Mennonite Seclusion." In *Anabaptism and Mission*, ed. Wilbert R. Shenk, 119-136. Scottdale, Pa.: Herald Press.

Vander Werff, Lyle L. 1977. *Christian Mission to Muslims: the Record*. Pasadena: William Carey Library.

Wakely, Mike. 1995. "A Critical Look at a New 'Key' to Evangelization." *EMQ* 31:152-162.

Watt, William Montgomery. 1991. *Muslim-Christian Encounters: Perceptions and Misperceptions*. London: Routledge.

Wenger, J. C., ed. 1956. *The Complete Writing of Menno Simons*. Scottdale, Pa.: Herald Press.

Wilson, J. Christy Jr. 1975. "Evangelization Where There Is Government Hostility." In *Let the Earth Hear His Voice*, ed. J. D. Douglas, 948-954. Minneapolis: World Wide Publications.

——. 1986. "The Legacy of Samuel M. Zwemer." *IBMR* 10:117-121.

——. 1989. "The Experience of Praying for Muslims." In *Muslims and Christians on the Emmaus Road*, ed. J. Dudley Woodberry, 323-336. Monrovia, Calif.: MARC.

——. 1996. "Costly Discipleship: Two Stories from Iran." *ERT* 20:152-155.

——. 1996. *More to be Desired than Gold*. 3d ed. South Hamilton, Mass.: Gordon-Conwell Theological Seminary.

Yoder, John H., ed. and trans. 1973. *The Legacy of Michael Sattler*. Scottdale, Pa.: Herald Press.

——. 1983. "The Social Shape of the Gospel." In *Exploring Church Growth*, ed. Wilbert R. Shenk, 277-284. Grand Rapids: Eerdmans.

Youssef, Samir. 1997. "How to Reach Muslims with the Message of Jesus Christ." Private paper, January. Surrey, B.C.

Zwemer, Samuel M. 1924. *The Law Of Apostasy in Islam*. London.

——. 1949. "Francis of Assisi and Islam (1182?-1226)." *MW* 39:247-251.

Annotated Bibliography

Christian Witness Among Muslims: A Handbook Written Especially for Christians in Africa (South Of Sahara). Achimota, Ghana: Africa Christian Press, 1971.

This short book (96 pp.) emerges from the African experience of witness among Muslims. Its gentle spirit and friendly attitude toward Muslims is combined with a confident conviction that Jesus Christ is Saviour and Lord of all people. No single author is indicated, because the contents of the book are the result of thousands of discussions with Muslims and Christians in sub-Saharan Africa.

Cooper, Anne, comp. *Ishmael My Brother: A Christian Introduction to Islam*. 2nd. ed. Tunbridge Wells, England: MARC, 1993.

This book is useful as a general introduction to Islam for Christians. It starts with the question of the Christian approach to other faiths, explains the basics of Islam in ten chapters, and sketches the Christian response. *Ishmael* could work well for a small group study, or even for a Bible college short course on Islam. Each chapter first states its objectives and provides a great resource list for each theme (317 pp.).

Cragg, Kenneth. *Jesus and the Muslim: An Exploration*. London: George Allen & Unwin, 1985.

Is there another book which brings together a love for Muslims, a knowledge of their religion, and a deep commitment to Jesus Christ as well as this one does? Kenneth Cragg is famous for presenting the beliefs and practices of Muslims in an empathetic way (such as in his *Call of the Minaret* as well as other books). It is perhaps not so well-known that he judges all he sees in that religion by the cross of Christ. This book is also a deeply Anabaptist reading of the behavior of Jesus when tempted—in contrast, as Cragg notes, to the corresponding decisions of the prophet of Islam (315 pp.).

Friesen, Leroy. *Mennonite Witness in the Middle East: A Missiological Introduction*. Elkhart, Ind.: Mennonite Board of Missions, 1992.
Mennonites have been meeting Muslims, Jews, and the ancient Christian communities in the Middle East for over a hundred years, but especially since World War II they have done so through such agencies as Mennonite Central Committee and Mennonite Board of Missions. Leroy Friesen documents that interaction, then provides a careful analysis and evaluation. He does not hesitate to criticize Mennonite efforts, but his approach is basically positive in a carefully thought-out proposal toward a "Theology of Mennonite Work in the Middle East" (160 pp.).

Goldsmith, Martin. *Islam and Christian Witness*. 3d ed. Bromley, Kent, England: OM Publishing, 1991.
This book is a fine representative of the genre of witness guides written out of the experiences of evangelical missionaries serving in Muslim settings. Goldsmith includes general information about Islam and the gospel, as well as tips for effective witnessing. His section on "dialogue" is sensible and sound. Goldsmith is a British professor who served in Southeast Asia (159 pp.). Other worthwhile contributions to this genre include the books of William Miller (Iran), Charles Marsh (North Africa), James Dretke (West Africa), and Jens Christensen (Central Asia).

Guillaume, Alfred., trans. *The Life of Muhammad*. (A translation of Ishaq's *Sirat Rasul Allah*). Karachi: Oxford University Press, 1955.
Ibn Hisham's edition of Ibn Ishaq's *Sirat Rasul Allah* is one of the earliest biographies of Muhammad. Guillaume's English translation reveals that early Muslims were quite comfortable with the portrait of a leader who participated in raids, military battles, and the assassination of opponents. This narrative comes entwined with the consistent claim that what happened in the life of the Prophet of Islam was the work of God himself (815 pp.).

Hahn, Ernest. *How to respond to Muslims*. St. Louis, Mo.: Concordia Publishing House, 1995.
This booklet (61 pp.) contains chapters on Islam and Muslims, Muslim presence in North America, comparison of Muslim and Christian beliefs, and tips for effective Christian witness among Muslims. Ernest Hahn writes out of intimate experience of Islam in South India. He has

been giving useful, trustworthy advice for many years in North America. This would make a good booklet to purchase in quantity for a congregation.

Hiebert, Paul G. *Anthropological Reflections on Missiological Issues*. Grand Rapids, Mich.: Baker Books, 1994.

Paul Hiebert is a Mennonite Brethren anthropologist. He was one of the first to draw the attention of contemporary evangelicals to the spiritual dimension of mission (what he coined the "excluded middle"). More recently he has been trying to moderate extreme views. Both contributions are reflected in this collection of well-written and interesting articles. "Biblical Perspectives on Spiritual Warfare" and "Healing and the Kingdom" are essential on spiritual dynamics of ministry. His much-cited article "Critical Contextualization" is also included here (272 pp.).

Kateregga, Badru D., and David W. Shenk. *A Muslim and A Christian in Dialogue*. Scottdale, Pa.: Herald Press, 1997.

An African Muslim and a United States Mennonite missionary attempt to explain, in twelve chapters each, the basics of their respective faiths and practices. Since first published in Africa in 1980, this has been one of the most widely cited books on Muslim beliefs in evangelical circles. It models something significant about the evangelical Anabaptist approach: we enter into friendly and peaceable relationships with Muslims, and we confess the truth of the gospel with joy and confidence (179 pp.).

Mawdudi, S. Abul A'la. *Towards Understanding Islam*. Edited and translated by Kurshid Ahmad. Indianapolis: Islamic Teaching Center, 1977.

Of the many introductions to Islam written by believers and nonbelievers, Muslims would probably recommend Maududi's book over any other. A South Asian Muslim with a confident writing style, Maududi inspired the lay movement Jama'at-i-Islami and published his own accessible commentary on the Qur'an. Like most Muslims, he is not a modernist. He explains Muslim faith as it is and feels no need to justify it against Western Enlightenment canons of what religion should be (134 pp.).

McCurry, Don M., ed. *The Gospel and Islam: A 1978 Compendium.* Monrovia, Calif.: MARC, 1979.

This is a very interesting collection of papers which were presented at the 1978 North American Conference on Muslim Evangelization. Many of the papers applied insights from the social sciences to the challenges of evangelism and church planting in Muslim societies. For example, there is a foundation paper from Paul Hiebert on "The Gospel and Culture." There are also reports on "the comparative status of Christianity and Islam" in many parts of the world. A milestone in evangelical thinking about mission among Muslims (638 pp.).

Musk, Bill. *The Unseen Face of Islam: Sharing the Gospel With Ordinary Muslims.* Eastbourne, Sussex, England: MARC, 1989.

British pastor Bill Musk writes out of mission experience in Muslim contexts. He has organized what he has learned about occult activity in Middle Eastern Muslim settings into separate chapters on such subhjects as the "evil eye," charms and amulets, and attendance at tombs of Muslim "saints." He wants to show prospective Christian workers that this "face" of Islam needs to be taken into account in attempts to witness among Muslims. *The Uneven Face* is a helpful, interesting, and readable book (315 pp.).

Nazir-Ali, Michael. *Islam: A Christian Perspective.* Exeter, England: Paternoster Press, 1983.

Here is one of the finest books on Islam from an Asian church leader. Nazir-Ali is from a convert family in Pakistan and writes with a special appreciation for Muslim cultures, especially in South Asia. He gives a very interesting presentation of the development of Islam and doesn't hesitate to describe daily realities such as Muhammad veneration. His comments on the local church, the foreign missionary, and the Muslim convert should be required reading for any church or mission which would like to minister in the Muslim world (185 pp.).

Newbigin, Lesslie. *The Gospel in a Pluralist Society.* Grand Rapids, Mich.: Eerdmans, 1989.

At the end of the twentieth century, many Westerners, including some Christians, tend to pose hard questions to missionaries who work to make disciples for Jesus Christ from among Muslims. The simple *fact* of religious plurality in Western societies has also made the *philosophy* of pluralism irresistible to some. Newbigin, out of forty years of mission among Hindus in India, takes the difficult questions head on and makes a strong case for the confidence that Christ is unique Lord and Savior (252 pp.).

Parshall, Phil. *Bridges to Islam: A Christian Perspective on Folk Islam.* Grand Rapids, Mich.: Baker, 1983.
Phil Parshall is one of the best-known evangelical writers on mission among Muslims. He has applied insights from the social sciences and Church Growth theory to Muslim contexts; in this case, popular Islam. He is concerned to "contextualize" the gospel for Muslims. Parshall's books have given many workers hope that traditional obstacles to witness among Muslims can be overcome, and "bridges" can be built. In recent years this kind of writing has opened up a discussion about theological integrity and unwarranted reliance on technique (161 pp.).

Rippin, Andrew. *Muslims: Their Religious Beliefs and Practices.* Vol. 1, The Formative Period. London: Routledge, 1990.
Many books provide the story of Muslim origins as Muslims themselves conceive it. Rippin's book stands out because, along with the Muslim version, it provides a historical context for those claims. A number of leading Western historians of Islam question the reliability of the traditional accounts of Muslim origins, including the collection of the Qur'an and the biography of Muhammad. It can be helpful for workers among Muslims to gain the perspective on Muslim tradition which such careful, scholarly studies provide (155 pp.).

Shenk, Calvin E. *Who Do You Say That I Am? Christians Encounter Other Religions.* Scottdale, Pa.: Herald Press, 1997.
This is a major Mennonite contribution to the discussion of the church's response to a plurality of religious commitments. Shenk provides a good description and analysis of exclusivism, inclusivism, and pluralism. He also carefully reviews the biblical teaching on other religions and on the person of Christ. Shenk has written out of extensive experience among Muslims in Ethiopia as well as more recent experience in interfaith contexts in Jerusalem. His last chapter gathers the peaceable threads found throughout the book and weaves them into a beautiful statement on "Understanding," "Respect," "Humility," and "Vulnerability" (304 pp.).

Shenk, David W. *Global Gods: Exploring the Role of Religions in Modern Societies.* Scottdale, Pa.: Herald Press, 1995.
David Shenk's chapter on Islam, and his unique presentation of gospel faith among the world religions, make this a very worthwhile book to

have on hand. Shenk establishes a reasonable framework by which to evaluate the religions at the start of his book, and then he takes the freedom to question whether various aspects of religion are helpful for the world today. Shenk begins some theological reflections on Islam and what he calls "the flight from suffering" (the *hijrah*) which are basic to an Anabaptist approach to Muslim faith (404 pp.).

Shenk, Wilbert W., ed. *Anabaptism and Mission*. Scottdale, Pa.: Herald Press, 1984.

This is an important resource for understanding the importance of evangelism in Anabaptist mission activity today. Wilbert Shenk has collected many of the seminal scholarly articles on the missionary vision and activity of the early Anabaptists. The 1946 paper by Franklin Littell is here, as well as a fine essay by Hans Kasdorf, "The Anabaptist Approach to Mission." But the most interesting articles are the historical studies of three European scholars, one of whom laments a movement from missionary zeal to "Mennonite seclusion" (264 pp.).

————, ed. *Exploring Church Growth*. Grand Rapids: Eerdmans, 1983.

This collection contains one of the most important pieces by Mennonites on mission among Muslims, David Shenk's "The Muslim Umma and the Growth of the Church." Shenk attempts to explore how Church Growth theory would play out in Muslim contexts. He combines strong affirmation of evangelism and the growth of the church with a critique of thinking which departs from biblical method and motivation.

Stacey, Vivienne. *Christ Supreme Over Satan: Spiritual Warfare, Folk Religion and the Occult*. Lahore, Pakistan: Masihi Isha'at Khana, 1986.

Vivienne Stacey, a fine British missionary, writes out of experiences in Pakistan and the Arabian Peninsula. She sees that in the life of ordinary Muslims there is a high occult component associated with "folk Islam." Stacey then gives some solid teaching from Scripture about victory over evil spirits in Jesus Christ (134 pp.). There is something wise, sensible, and balanced about her perspective.

Woodberry, J. Dudley, ed. *Muslims and Christians on the Emmaus Road*. Monrovia, Calif.: MARC, 1989.

This book is a collection of papers presented in 1987 at a conference sponsored by the Lausanne Committee for World Evangelization. The themes are organized according to the parts of the story of Jesus' postresurrection encounter with two disciples. Kenneth Cragg, Colin Chapman, and Dudley Woodberry contribute important papers. There is continuing discussion of social science insights, but also scriptural themes and the dynamics of spiritual conflict. There are interesting first-person accounts of witnessing in various contexts. Paul Hiebert's "Power Encounters and Folk Islam" is part of this collection (394 pp.).

LINCOLN CHRISTIAN COLLEGE AND SEMINARY

The Author

Gordon D. Nickel was born in Vancouver, B.C., and lives in Alberta, where he is doing research toward a Ph.D. in Quranic Studies. After spending high school years in South India as the son of missionaries, he studied at Columbia Bible Institute and the Universities of British Columbia and Saskatchewan.

For six years Nickel was associate editor of *Mennonite Brethren Herald*. He then completed master's degrees at Mennonite Brethren Biblical Seminary as well as the School of Oriental and African Studies in London, England.

Between 1986 and 1996, Nickel and his wife Gwenyth were missionaries under MBMS International, including five years in Karachi, Pakistan. Nickel also taught missions and anthropology at Bethany Bible Institute (Hepburn, Sask.) from 1994-1998.

Gordon and Gwenyth have three children: Matthew (1979), Amalia (1981), and Daniel (1984). They are attendees at and members of Dalhousie Mennonite Brethren Community Church in Calgary. They are also members of Eigenheim Mennonite Church in Rosthern, Saskatchewan.

266.97
N6322

99703

LINCOLN CHRISTIAN COLLEGE AND SEMINARY

3 4711 00153 6392